TELL WORLD I'D HOPED TO SEE IT WITH YOU

A COLLECTION OF POETRY BY Kristina Mahr

Copyright © 2022 Kristina Mahr

All rights reserved.

ISBN-13: 979-8362471361

*"You are not as tired of the poem
As I am of the memory."*

- Jericho Brown -

AUTHOR'S NOTE

The poems within this collection span six years of love and loss, heartbreak and healing. They are my greatest hits, by which I mean, the greatest hits my heart has taken. Putting them into words helped. Putting those words on paper and sharing them with all of you helped even more. I have no way to know how things might have played out over this stretch of time if not for the existence of poetry, but I feel sure I would have been worse for it. I am grateful for poetry, grateful for words, grateful for you.

These poems are arranged chronologically, so in reading them in order, you will truly be on this journey with me.

I'll see you on the other side.

kristina mahr

I Pretend

I pretend that my heartbeats don't thud.

I pretend that I don't feel them,
that it's business as usual
inside of my chest.

I pretend that my smiles are more
than just gritted teeth.

I pretend that I mean them,
that they curve with something more like joy
and less like sadness.

I pretend that the world applauds,
that I take my bows,
that you

— *that you* —

are in the audience,
throwing flowers onto the stage
where I pretend that I am fine.

What It Doesn't Say

I am at war with the voice
inside my head.

The one that says,
"Nobody can drown you
if you don't let them
close enough
to hold your head under."

Because what it doesn't say
is that nobody can
save you then, either.

Break Down

We didn't break up
so much as we broke down.
We ran out of power,
out of hope,
out of remembering
what it was
that we were fighting for.

For Me

Truth be told,
what makes this hard
is I wish I had not seen
how hard you fight
for everything you love
when you did not fight for me.

Later

I am a sea,
an ocean,
an entire goddamn universe
of unsaid words.

I saved them all for later.

(I thought we had a later.)

What I Deserve

"You deserve more"
is code for
"I don't want to try to be what you deserve."

It's code for
"I'm pretending this is for you
when really I'm just scared."

It's code for
"You deserve someone who stays,
and I'm about to be
the very opposite of that."

That Scene

I've stopped playing that scene through in my mind.

The one where you come back.

Now I play the one where you stay gone
and I move forward
and I'm happier than I was ever going to be
in the one where you come back.

Ferry

Sometimes when I close my eyes,
we're still sitting there,
on that ferry,
and I'm still shivering beneath your coat,
and you're still pointing out the stars,
but this time when the boat docks,
we don't get off.
We listen to the dolphins chatter,
and we watch the waves dance,
and we are safe
from everything that came next.

Demons

Your demons have never
played well with mine.

Yours push
(me away,)
mine pull
(you closer.)

Yours fight for air
while mine gladly drown.

Yours are already looking
ahead, ahead, ahead,
while mine can't stop looking
at you.

As Though

They told me to follow my heart,
but I kept ending up on your doorstep.

"Stop," they said.
"Follow it somewhere else."

As though there are pieces
in other places.

As though I rationed it.

As though all of it
isn't yours.

As though I planned ahead for a time
when all of it was yours
but I was not.

I Think I Used To

I think I used to love you,
though the reasons are fading
under the weight of your absence.
Under the weight of your apologies
where they fell flat against my ears,
across my back,
crushing and crippling and cruel,
twenty, thirty, forty lashes
for a crime I did not commit.
How dare you tell me
that you were doing this for me.

The Kind I Cannot Win

I stay up late sometimes
and play a game,
the kind I should not play.

I think of things you said
and try to decipher
truths from lies.

Some nights I make them all lies
and fall asleep hating you.

Other times I make them all truths
and fall asleep missing you.

It's the kind of game
I should not play
because it's the kind I cannot win.

Boy of a Man

What a boy of a man you are,
with your half-formed wings
and your reckless smile.
With your penchant for running
and never looking back,
never looking back.
With your sunshine laugh
and your moonlit apologies,
pouring whiskey down your throat
like life can't touch you,
like love can't touch you,
like I can't touch you.
What a boy of a man you are,
not watching where you go,
not watching when I go,
howling at the moon
and spinning circles 'round the sun
like what you do
doesn't break hearts,
doesn't break souls,
doesn't break *my* heart,
doesn't break *my* soul.
Like we,
like this,
like you
aren't doomed.

Just a Little Bit

This hallway is full of open doors,
and I keep trying the locked one.

My fists are dripping blood,
and the hallway is filling with fire,
but I can't stop pounding at this door.

Save yourself,
says my brain,
for it is whole and sure.

Never stop knocking,
even if it hurts,
says my heart,
for it is still just a little bit broken.

This Is What I Remember

This is what I remember:
it was raining,
and you were driving,
and I could not look at you.

This is what I remember:
it was raining,
and I was crying,
and you asked me
to please say something.

This is what I remember,
this is what I remember,
this is what I remember:
it was raining,
and I hugged you goodbye
outside the airport,
and when I walked away,
I didn't look back.

I Thank You

You left more kindly
than you ever stayed
mostly because
you never came back.
I almost don't know how to fall asleep upon
a pillow that's not wet,
but I'm learning,
and I thank you
for knowing that I did not know
how to be the one to go.

Bittersweet

It was not everything
over the span of a life,
but it was everything
over the span of those months,
and it was something
over the span of my life.

It is not the end all, be all,
except for the times that it was.

It is past-tense verbs
and bittersweet now,
memories
and patchwork hearts.

It is
and then it was.

It should've been
and then it wasn't.

It always will
even though it never will be again.

Already Gone

There is tape hanging from your ceiling,
and your fan is two speeds too high.

If you shook me, I would rattle,
full of words I cannot fathom into sentences.

But instead, you hold me,
and I miss you,
even though you're there.

But instead, you hold me,
and I miss you,
because I know
you're already gone.

All I Take Back

A hundred thousand songs
about broken hearts,
and I still don't understand
how anyone survives it.

(How does anyone survive it?)

Forget me, forget me,
you said,
as you carved your name into my bones.

I take all of it back,
I take none of it back,
all I take back is
every time I ever apologized
for wanting more from you than silence.

Every Night

I'm not the praying kind,
but every night,
I ask the stars to keep you safe.

Can you see them where you are?

Do they tell you about me?

Do they tell you
that my dreams are coming true,
but that when my mind wanders,
it's still always straight to you?

Bent

I thought that we were bent;
you decided we were broken.

You decided, you decided,
everything turned on you deciding.

You decided I wasn't worth
whatever this was going to take.

Life is made up of choices,
and I have learned to be grateful
for everyone who chooses to stay,
even when it's hard
(especially when it's hard.)

"Do you still miss him?"
they ask me,
and I am teaching myself
to lie.

What I Wanted

I never wanted you
to be
anyone other than
who you are.
I just wanted
the you who you are
to want
the me who I am.

Let Me Show You

Tell me about the morning you woke up
and decided you didn't want to hear the ends
to any of my stories.

(I have never stopped wanting to hear the ends to yours.)

I am filling my hands
with other things now.

Keeping them busy,
keeping them here.

This is the way you left me.

Stop closing your eyes,
let me show you –
these unfinished stories,
these empty hands.

This is the way you left me.

Stop closing your eyes,
let me show you.

How

How imperfect we were,
how razor-burned
and tear-stained.
How broken-wished
and phone call-missed,
how forgotten,
how misremembered.
How far gone,
how lost, unfounded,
how dreamt,
how felt,
how wanted.
How none of it,
not one of it,
not one heartbroken drop of it,
matters
in the face of
how I loved you.

Ships in the Night

We were only ever meant to be
ships in the night,
only meant to cross paths
and continue on our way,
but we threw ropes across
from your deck to mine
and my deck to yours,
and we held on for dear life.

Until the storms blew through and frayed them,
until the sun came up and blinded us,
until you started looking off toward the horizon.

You dropped the ropes and sailed away,
and I looked down at the blisters on my hands
and suddenly remembered –

there was somewhere else I was supposed to be.

My Happy Place

My happy place is a couch
beside a Christmas tree,
long after the season's passed.

I read you all of the words on my skin,
and you compare the sizes of our hands.

I want to tell you then
that though mine are small,
I know they can hold multitudes,
but the memory turns black and blue
when I'm reminded of the truth –

these hands could not even hold you.

Something Lasting

I'm sorry you dated a writer.

The blood can be dried,
just like it is,
and I will cut the wound back open
and root around inside of it
to pull out the memory of how it felt.

You can be gone,
just like you are,
and I will pull you back
to watch you leave me
again,
and again,
and all over again,
so I can turn it into words.

I can be fine,
just like I am,
and I will picture your face
and remember your voice in my ear
until my heart breaks all over again,
just so I can put it down in ink,
just so I can carve it into stone –

just so I can try to create something lasting
in a world where nothing ever lasts.

Reclaim It

I reclaim the shape of my heart
from hands that did not know how to hold it.

That crushed,
that dropped,
that forgot.

That didn't call,
that didn't write —

hands attached to bodies
claimed by boys
who looked like men
who ran
and didn't look back
and haven't looked back
and won't look back
and I —

I reclaim the shape of my heart
from anyone
who did not think it mattered.

The Better Question

When I close my eyes,
I'm walking backward,
and you are walking forward.

I'm rewinding,
I'm unspooling,
I'm only where I've already been.

When I close my eyes,
you're out of sight,
you were never even in it.

People still ask me
how you are,
and I think the better question
is who.

These Words

These words are still about you,
but they're no longer for you.
They are pulled from my bones,
and you cannot have them.

The Only One, the Lonely One

In my head you miss me
and you wish things could be different.

Don't tell me if it isn't true.

I'm still blindly groping
the walls within me
for a switch I don't have.
An off switch,
a stop switch,
a pick up the pieces and run switch.

We both lost things
in this fire we set,
so why am I the only one trying to find them?

(The only one, the lonely one.)

If you're standing in the middle of the street,
screaming,
and nobody hears you,
are you really even here at all?

Seashells

The waves whisper promises to the shore,
but then they leave,
but then they leave,
but then they leave.

We built sandcastles at low tide,
and everything was swept away by morning.

Don't you see?

You were born of the sand
and the salt
and the sea,
and I am just a girl
collecting seashells
to remind me that I was once here.

Nothing Here

I have nothing here of you
but my own two hands that touched you,
but my own two eyes that saw you,
(that saw you see me,)
but my one lonely heart that loved you.

I have nothing here of you
but a raging in my ears
and a howling in my blood
and a rampant wish

that I cannot wish

for this to be

undone.

Hourglass

This hourglass ran out of sand
so long ago now,
and I cannot flip it over.

I joke that time stopped for me
the day you left,
and it's the kind of joke
where no one laughs
because I think I tell it wrong.

I spread my arms to walk the line
between my present and our past.

People ask me where I'm going,
as though I'm not already gone.

I Exist

Tell me again how sorry you are;
I need something empty
in which to store my hopes.

Stop pretending you want things you don't.

(Stop whispering my name in my dreams.)

I still remember the exact tilt of your head
when you said you didn't see another way.

As though things don't exist
if you refuse to see them.

As though things don't exist
if you
pretend
they don't.

Flattened

It's hot in here,
and I'm draped in layers
of months since I heard
your voice.

How stifling, how suffocating,
how is it that
it gets heavier instead of lighter?

Each second an ounce,
each minute a pound,
each hour another crack
in my bones.

I am flattened,
I am floored

by all that could have
been.

I Cannot

I press my ear to the wall,
and I discover
that silence has its own sound.

Like a rush, like a roar,
like everything
you ever said to me
and everything
you never said to me
echoing through my veins.

The end of the year is coming,
and I cannot
take you
with me.

Hope

People ask me
what the hell
I'm still
holding onto,
and I tell them
hope.

What If

What if you
chase your dreams
and I
chase my dreams
and we promise
to look up
every now and then
to see if our dreams
have brought us
close enough
to one another
to reach out
and touch.

Less Joy

Sometimes I lose sight
of where I wanted to go from here,
but then I realize
my eyes are closed.

Stop time,
rewind,
let me do it all again.

We may make more sense apart,
but oh,
we also make
less joy.

What If You Came Back

What if you came back
and
we straightened
the crooked parts
and
I didn't push but
you didn't pull
and
we didn't hide
from the rain
and
you didn't forget
me
and
we were the people
we used to be
instead of the people
we are now
with chisel fingertips
and hammer heartbeats
and your hand
over my mouth
and my scars
on your hands
and –
what if you came back.

Save Me

I did not mind that you were sand;
I built a house on you all the same.

Look, our floor is made of
sand dollars and starfish,
fragile and alive.

I tiptoe around them
but you break more and more each day.

A message in a bottle
floated through last week,
with a note that just said,
"Save me."

It floated through,
is what you said.

And I didn't ask
why it looked as though
you were about to
throw it out to sea.

Kites

You say that you love
flying kites,
but what you love
is watching the wind catch hold of them
and carry them as high as you have string,
and then letting go of the string
and walking away.

Nobody's Better

The past is bloodied,
dripping red,
its skin is buried
beneath
my fingernails.

My arms are months long,
my heart is never here.

Nobody's better,
nobody's ever been better,
at holding on

to what's

long gone.

Everything

You don't know
me at all
if you think
I'd walk away
from a door
just because it's closed.

Not when everything
I want
is on the other side.

Not until I've tried
everything.

And everything includes
waiting patiently
for you
to open it.

But It Was

Today I came back to
a hole where
a home had been,
so I made a bed
of all the rubble.

There is gravel digging
into my spine,
ashes falling
in my eyes.

They tell me to move,
to build a home somewhere new,
like they're telling me
it's a quarter past two.

(Like it's obvious.)

(Like I'm a fool.)

Like a hole is not a home.

And I'm whispering, *"But it was."*

No Promises

I told you that
one of my biggest fears
is the ocean at night.

The way it seems endless,
but you know it must end.

The way your eyes
play tricks on you.

The way you see things
beneath the surface
that are not there.

I am less scared of the ocean now
than I am of you.

(The ocean makes no promises.)

All I Ever Seem to Do

I've never been able
to keep my head above
love.

To float in it,
to swim in it.

All I ever seem to do
is drown in it.

(I Needed You.)

I am a better person now
than I was with you,
but I'm also a better person now
than I was before you.

(I needed you.)

To break me so I
could rebuild me.

(I needed you.)

I Didn't Mean To

I've cried wolf so many times,
I'm not sure anybody's
listening anymore.

(Are you still listening?)

Somebody asked me
to draw a picture
of hope,
and I drew a hand
reaching out
through the darkness
for mine.

I drew an anchor,
I drew a buoy.

And I didn't mean to,
I didn't mean to,
but —

I drew you.

Only One

In the grand scheme of things,
you were only one raindrop
in the middle of a thunderstorm,
but you were the raindrop
that slipped through a crack
in the skylight on my bedroom ceiling
and landed on my cheek.

(You were the raindrop that woke me.)

Remember

I had such a hard time
forgetting,
but that's nothing compared to
how hard
it's become
to remember.

Safe Mode

If anyone asks,
I restarted in
Safe Mode
instead of
Normal Mode.

I was shut down
improperly.

Nothing was saved.

I don't know
how to do this
anymore.

Doomed

You will hear in the silence
that I don't love you anymore,
but I wanted you to know
in this small place
just outside the silence
that the truth is,
loving you
has spread
to my bones,
and I am doomed,
doomed,
doomed.

That's What I Wanted to Tell You

You say the past can't hurt me,
and I wonder why it is
that my memories come with daggers
when yours don't.

I guess I paid extra for these.

(In blood, in tears.)

I've thought about this,
the things I want to tell you,
the way I want to tell you.
I've thought about this –
about how my heart weighs more now,
and how it used to drag me
oceans deep,
but I learned to swim,
or, I guess,
I learned to drown
without the burning.

If my heart weighs more now,
it's because you filled it.

That's what I wanted to tell you.

It Knew

Hold onto me.

(I mean it.)

I was built from
friction
and flight,
and I'm going to try
to run.

Sometimes I think about the fact that
you are the only one
who will ever be able to say
you had my heart
when it was whole.

I understand now,
what it was doing.

The way it fell in love
kicking
and
screaming.

The way it knew,
it knew,
it knew.

(It knew better.)

Ghosts

They keep reaching for me,
even as I bat their hands away.

Maybe it's because
I also beg them to come closer.

I'm so much of a push and a pull outside,
I'm so much of the same inside.

I live with ghosts.

(I won't let them leave.)

Heartbreak

I think the world is swimming more
in heartbreak
than in ocean water.

I search faces for it.

I look for shatters
behind smiles,
wounds that needed stitches
wrapped in bandages instead.

(Because it's the best that they could do.)

(We're all doing the best that we can do.)

A Weakness

I have a weakness, still,
for you,
in a hard shift,
in a dizzying change,
like the earth is all the same,
it just started spinning
the other way.
In the way loving you
was a strength
just yesterday.

I Go, Too

I know what I said,
but then I slammed my finger
in the drawer,
and instead of a curse,
I screamed your name.

(I know I said that I was fine.)

I stomp, though,
and the rafters shake,
and the birds fly away,
and nothing,
nothing,
stays.

(I go, too.)

You will see me
and think that I'm still here,
but I

go,

too.

The Things Worth Keeping

I still lean back.

Even as my feet
carry me forward,
I lean back.

I have to keep reminding myself
that you're not back there.

If anything,
you're ahead.

You're when
we're both a little older
and both a little wiser
and both know a little better

how to hold onto
the things
worth keeping.

Coming to Terms

I have come to terms with the fact that
there will always be a knot
in the middle of this necklace,
in the same way there will always be knots
in my veins and arteries,
where the blood doesn't flow quite right,
where my pulse scatters and scrambles,
where missing you has made
a mess of my insides.

I have come to terms with the fact that
we have nothing more to say,
but oh how badly
I still want
to hear
your voice.

That's All There Is

Someday someone
may find these words,
but it won't be somewhere romantic
like a bottle in the ocean
or a tin can buried under a tree.

They'll just be scratched on a pad of paper
next to my bed
or on an internet search of my name
or love
or heartbreak.

I'm creating this record,
every day,
of how someone will see
what you were to me.

Here, I'll make this easier –
I loved him.

That's all there is.

Good to You

Summer has a sway,
and I don't recognize you in it.
You shudder like winter,
you flourish like spring,
you wilt like fall.
You don't give
more than you're sure
you can take back.
I wanted you to sink a little,
not to slice any major arteries,
but maybe to nick a vein.
To bleed a little.
I'm covered in bandages
and scars,
and all I wanted
was a single drop
of your blood.
All I wanted
was something
in the face of my
everything.
And anyway,
this is all to say,
I hope the summer's
good to you.
I hope all of life
is good to you.
(I would've been so good to you.)

And Yet, and Still

I know everything
there is to know now,
and yet,
and still,
I just wanted to say,
I miss you.
I know every reason not to,
and yet,
and still,
I don't think
I'll ever
stop.

Wrecking Ball

You agree that you're
a wrecking ball,
but
you say
a wrecking ball
can't cause any damage

unless

it's

pushed.

I Smile Like This

He asks me why I smile like this,
like it hurts,
and it stops me in my tracks
because nobody else
seems to have noticed
that my smile broke
when my heart did.

There's a drawer in my dresser
that I keep locked,
and I can tell that it bothers him.

(I never told him about you.)

It'll probably slip out some day,
in my sleep or in a scream.

In a scream in my sleep.

It'll probably slip out some day.

Until then,
I smile like this.

Gritted teeth
like prison bars
for your name.

I smile like this.

Sieve

How am I?
Oh, I have
more holes in me
than I did.
I'm a little more sieve,
a little less contained,
a little less
whole,
a little more
drained.
A little more
and a little less
as one day turns into
the next.
Hold me over a garden.
Maybe something will grow
from all that I used to be.

Unforgivable

Tell me the things that are unforgivable.

I keep thinking I've found them,
but then I lose them.

(But then I forgive them.)

Tell me where this ends.

Does this end?

Every time I think it has,
it's only a break, only a pause.

Only a moment to inhale
before the next breath comes out rasping,
panting,
losing a race I never wanted to run.

I just wanted you to stay.

That's it, that's all.

I just wanted you to stay.

(That isn't it, that isn't all.)

(I just wanted you to love me.)

The Only Story

I think I should start with once upon a time,
but it feels wrong without an end that's
happily ever after.

Still, there was you,
and there was me,
and that in itself feels like
once upon a time.

It feels like a fairytale
written by someone
who'd been in love
but lost.

Someone who didn't know
how to write
anything but goodbye.

Anyway, once upon a time
I loved you.

It's the only story
I've ever wanted to tell.

It's Like This

I am lost,
and everyone knows it,
but they don't know
it's like this.

Like a maze with no exits
and your goodbye
in my ears.

They don't know
it's like this.

Tell Me

Tell me how I live within your memories.

Do I live well?
Do I laugh often?
Do I make you laugh often?

Are there tears in there?

(If there aren't, I wonder what you did with them.)

Am I pretty in them,
do I shine in them,
do I want too much in them?

Is there an alley where you kiss me,
a couch where you trace the curve of my ear,
do you pretend,
pretend,
pretend in them?

(Do you pretend you love me in them?)

Tell me, do I breathe within your memories.

Tell me, do I stand a chance within your memories.

Tell me,
was I ever more
than temporary
in your memories.

Tell me how I live within your memories.

Silent

It is hard for me to love someone
who has a voice
but chooses to stay silent.

Someone Else

It's all someone else now.

(Does that bother you?)

Someone else loves me.

Someone else
knows all
my secrets.

All of the quiet things
I'd never told anyone
but you.

I tell him now.

(Does that bother you?)

Truth be told —

(it bothers me.)

For You

I am for you.

Do you hear me,
do you hear me.

(I've always wondered if you hear me where you are.)

Not can, I know you can,
but I wonder if you do.

It doesn't matter.

I am for you,
whether you know it or feel it or want it
or not.

My heartbeats thud
like everybody else's,
but in each thud they say
your name.

And no matter
how hard I scrub,
if you dust me for fingerprints,
they're yours.

So if you ever feel
like the world is against you,
just remember –

I am for you.

Except, Perhaps

Nothing hurts me more
than the things you never said,

except, perhaps, for the things
that you said but never meant.

Razed

I've been razed before.
Rebuilt from floor to ceiling.
He stops by one day and says,
"I used to live here.
I'd love to see what you've done with the place."
And I am so often foolish,
I let him in.
I show him how I've been redone,
how the beams are sturdier,
how the foundation no longer caves.
But he,
he finds
every false wall,
all of the hidden rooms,
where I keep his laugh,
his fingertips,
his smile,
and a shot for shot remake
of the day he left me.
He watches it play,
I watch it with him.
(Though I have it memorized.)
And he turns to me
and smiles and says,
"It won't be like that again."

I've been razed before.

Rebuilt from floor to ceiling.

(But I am so often foolish.)

On a Beach

I think we're on a beach somewhere.

I think you're surfing
while I write,
while I glance up
from time to time
and look for you
in the waves.

I think you call for me,
you hold your hand out to me,
and I laugh and shake my head.

But then I think I put my pen down
and go to you.

I think I swim to you.

I think I love you.

(I know I loved you.)

But there, I think I still do.

A Hell of a Thing

My walls are covered
in pictures of what was.

What's been.

What will never be again.

I take them down every night,
I hang them up again every morning.

I can't stand the empty walls.

Everyone says empty
means the potential to be filled,
but all I see is empty.

It's a hell of a thing,
the way someone comes and fills
what you hadn't known was empty.

It's a hell of a thing,
the way they leave,
and now you can't forget it.

Your Heart

Tell me about your heart.

Does it howl at night like mine.

Do you listen to it.

Does it only ever beat,
or does it thud,
or does it pound.

Do you remember
where you got
that scar.

Do you remember
why you built
that wall.

Is it soft.

Is it stone.

Was any of it ever mine.

Backpack

A psychic once told me
I could go ahead and love you
but that you'd always be leaving.

He said you had a backpack on,
and you kept your heart inside of it.

He warned me not to let you
stick my heart in there, too,
but it's too late for that,

far too late for that,

I snuck it in there myself when you weren't looking.

Show it the open road, will you.
Show it the mountains,
show it freedom,
show it why I gave it to you in the first place.

Show it I wasn't wrong about you.

And someday, someday –

give it back.

Hello, World

Pull me up by the roots, would you.

Love me for the way
I reach for the sky
even when
I'm cold,
even when
I'm empty.

Carve your initials
in my skin
as a reminder
for when you go.

Let them whisper for you,
let them sing for you –

Hello world,
I was here.

Hello, world,
I loved her.

Hello, world,
I left her.

All You Did

I have this whole world inside of me,
and you set one foot on its shores
and closed your eyes
and pulled a hurricane from the sea.

And you left.

(You left.)

You tell everyone you've been here,
but all you did
was see it from afar and break it.

You with your wanderer's feet
and your careless hands.

All you did was break it.

These Scars

I am fewer bandages now,
less dripping blood,
fewer fractures,
smaller holes.

They still ask me about you, though.

Have I seen you,
have I heard your voice,
have I missed you,
missed you,
missed you.

(I have missed you,
missed you,
missed you.)

But I smile.

I show them scars
instead of scabs.

They look sorry for the scars,
but I refuse their pity.

I fought for these scars,
I bled for these scars,
I tried for these scars.

I loved for these scars.

Drain

He thinks I'm a waterfall,
but I'm just a faucet
someone forgot
to turn off.

I don't flow,
I just pour.

You wanted part of me?
You have all of me.
I don't know any other way.

(You do.)

I wanted all of you
and I have none of you.

My fault, my fault –
I thought you were a reservoir
but you were just
a drain.

Do You

I am never not trying
to fold myself into something
you can carry.

I file my edges so they can't tear
your pockets or your palms,
I shove cotton in my mouth
so I can't wake you up
with my screams,
I hold my breath
to be light as air
so you won't notice
the weight of me.

Do you love me yet.

I am soft
and quiet
and light.

Do you love me yet.

Over You

I'm so over you
so over you
so over being
under you
your thumb
your press
and waver
your certainty
about only
your uncertainty
the way you never
fought with me
or fought for me
or thought for one single second
that this is not for me
your I'm sorry
and I wish I could
so sorry
and I thought I might
and you're wonderful
you're wonderful
well nobody leaves wonderful
and I'm so over you
so over you
so over being
over you
so over being
not with you.

A World

I just want to live in a world where
only gentle hands reach
and only kind words meet the air.

Where embraces don't suffocate
and questions aren't accusations.

Where I can close my eyes
and not have to fear
that the walls will cave in while I sleep.

I guess I can make it simpler than that.

I just want to live in a world where you still love me.

I just want to live in a world where you never stop.

Still

We are still those people,
and so,
we can never be strangers.
It gives me comfort, that.
Wherever we go,
however far apart we drift,
I will always be the girl
looking up at you in that alley,
and you will always be the boy
who kissed me.

Waves

I haunt this shipwreck,
but I'm no siren.
I sing nobody closer, no,
I howl them all away.

Stop trying to save me,
stop trying to save me.

I am a tempest,
didn't you know.
I storm, now.
I rage.

Sunshine got me nowhere.
Still water carries nothing,
changes nothing.

It was waves that carried you away,
and I'm convinced, I'm convinced –

it'll be waves that carry you back.

If It Could

My shadow's growing longer.
I can't look at it without wondering
where your shadow is,
whose hand it's holding now.

The leaves are starting to fall.
I can't look at them without wondering
how they knew it was time to let go,
whether they tried at all to stay.

The morning breeze has begun to bite.
I can't feel it without wondering
whether I was always this cold,
whether I'll always be this cold.

The sun is setting earlier
and rising later,
and I want to hate it
for leaving me so often in the dark,
but I think that it would stay if it could.

I cannot say that for everything.

Remember Me

I have been forgotten before,
but I have never felt it like this.

Like I blink,
and you forget my favorite song,
and I blink,
and you forget the color of my eyes.

Like I blink,
and you forget the sound of my laugh,
and I blink,
and you forget that you ever loved me.

Like seconds and minutes and hours
and days
and days
and days pass,
and I am less than I once was,
because you are not here
to remember me.

Bulldozer

He carved his initials into my spine
just below mine
and now leaves don't grow here anymore.
Nothing grows here anymore.

Someone came with a bulldozer
and I kept waiting for him to chain himself to me,
but then I realized
he was the one driving it.

I guess I take up too much space.
I guess people are worried I'll fall
the next time it storms
and destroy everything around me.
I guess he's always wanted to yell timber,
always needed more kindling for his fire,
always wondered if something better
might grow here.

Or maybe he just saw something
he used to lean on
and didn't want to be reminded
that he used to need somewhere
to lean.

Phoenix

I do not know
what is supposed to rise
from all of these ashes,
but I suspect
it's going to be
me.

Our Blue Moon

What if that was it,
do you ever wonder if that was it.

Our chance,
our one in a million,
our blue moon
hole in one
scratch-off win.

The big one,
the best one,
the best we could do.

Did we do the best we could do.

Did we try,
did we really try,
did we look at each other,
did we really look at each other,
did we *see* each other.

Now that I can't see you anymore,
I can't help but wonder
if I ever really did.

California

Every other song I hear
is about California
and how the sun never stops shining there
and how everything's going to be better there.

I left my heart there.

I forgot to pack it with the rest of my things,
and you never sent it back,
and now I think it must be
lost in between your couch cushions
with all of the pennies and gum wrappers
that aren't worth anything to you either.

Everything's better in California, they sing.

It was, they're right, it was.

The trouble is,
I'm not there anymore.

The trouble is,
I'm never
   going
      back.

Not Yet

I always hope that
when you finally do turn back,
I'll be looking the other way.

What I'm trying to say is,
don't turn back yet.

What I'm trying to say is,
I'm not ready yet.

Isn't It Cruel

If I had one hundred lives to live,
I would want to live
every one of them with you.

And isn't it cruel,
isn't it cruel,
that the only one I get –

I have to live
   without
      you.

Your Ghost

Your ghost doesn't scare me.

I feel him just the same as I felt you,
a thousand miles away,
closest when my eyes are closed.

He is just as silent, just as sorry,
I can't touch him either.

The only difference
between you and him
is I do not think
he'll ever leave me.

Blame

I have spent long nights
walking back and forth
between our houses,
blame clenched tightly in my fists,
unsure upon whose doorstep
to lay it.

Here is what I have decided,
I have decided this:

it was my fault
for believing your words
instead of your actions.

It was your fault
   they never
      matched.

(Say It.)

I am scattered a little bit,
just a little bit everywhere,
did you see me in the sky last night,
I was there,
did you see me in your dreams last night,
I was there,
did you see me in a stranger last night,
I was there.

If I have to remember you,
you have to remember me.
I don't make the rules,
and in this, at least,
neither do you.

If you miss somebody, say it.

I miss you.

(Say it.)

What Has Changed

What has changed,
can I tell you what has changed.

(Me.)

Somebody new
runs his fingertip up my arm,
and I don't shiver,
I don't flinch,
no,
I don't feel it.

This armor, it is thick, and
can I tell you what has changed.

(Me.)

Hey, you didn't want me
when I was me.

Do you want me now
    that I
        am not.

Two Years Ago

Two years ago someone built a sandcastle
and I said it was beautiful
while you said you'd seen better.

I think that sums us up.

I have said goodbye to you so many times
I don't think you think I mean it.

(I don't.)

The calendar tells me when I should miss you.
It says you once loved me on this day,
and maybe there's a chance
you'll love me on this day again.

(You won't.)

I just thought that we were beautiful.

You just thought
   you could
      do better.

Hello, Love

I love you like last November,
and the one before.
Do you remember.
(I keep forgetting to forget.)
It shows up like clockwork
every morning,
like it missed the call
that said
this appointment is canceled.
It shows up and it waits.
I call it in,
I can't help it.
I say, hello, love.

Hello, love.

I'm sorry to say
that he
    is still
        not here.

I Could Have

The only thing I know
with any certainty
is that I cannot possibly
love you this much
forever.

But oh,
    I could have.

Every Poem

What the hell was that for.

(What the hell was all of this for.)

I wrote you a poem.

It's this one,
it's the one before,
it's the one that I know will come after.

I wrote you every poem.

I emptied all of my love into your bones,
but I had nowhere to empty my heartbreak.

So I wrote you every poem.

Someday I'm sure I will run out of heartbreak.

But I once thought that
   about
      love.

Forever

I will get over
so many parts of this,
so many of the cracks
and crevices
and scars,
but I will never get over
the fact that you did not mean
forever
when you said you loved me,
but you meant
forever
when you said goodbye.

A Handful of Roses

A handful of roses
survived the first frost,
and I can't help but wonder
if they would have fought so hard to hold on
had they known
that it's only the beginning,
that it will only get worse from here,
that they have
   no chance
      at all.

Happier

I am happier
more often
without you
than I was
with you,
it just never
reaches
    the same
        heights.

Hell If I Know

He asks me what love is,
and I say hell if I know.

Hell if I know.

I thought it was the way
you looked at me,
but now I think
it was only the way

I

looked at

you.

Kept

I kept the way you said my name.

I threw out most everything else,
but I could not part with that,
and I could not part with your arms around me,
and I will probably regret this later,
but I could not part with your laugh.

I swear, I swear,
I threw everything else away,
I threw
almost
everything else away.

(I kept the way I love you, too.)

(I have no idea how to part with that.)

Can't

He says
he can't
keep doing this,
and I ask what,
thinking maybe it's
waking up early
and maybe it's
going to bed late
and maybe it's
eating pizza every day,
and I ask what
because I don't know,
I don't see,
I have no idea that
the thing
he can't keep doing
is loving me.

The Foundation

I see now I should not
have made you the foundation.

Perhaps a wall,
perhaps a staircase,
perhaps perhaps
a ceiling.

Something that can crumble
without the rest of me

coming

down

too.

Still You

I no longer know
what the question is,
but I'm pretty sure
the answer is
still you.

Dead End

My mind is a maze

    and around every turn

is a dead end,

    which is to say,

around every turn

    is you.

Winter Solstice

The only thing different
about today
is that I have fewer hours
to miss you in the sunshine
and more
to miss you
in the dark.

Waiting

Sometimes love
is not
what wakes
you up.

Sometimes it's just
there waiting
for when
you do.

Better

I have been made helpless by you
in better ways than this

and I have reached for you
with hands that shook
for better reasons than this

and I,
and I,
have always deserved

better

than

this.

But Mostly

Sometimes I turn over
memories in my head,
and I think,
I should have kissed you then,
and I should have touched you then,
and I should have held you more tightly then.

But mostly I turn over
just one memory in my head,
and I think,
you shouldn't
   have left
      me then.

It Has Taken Some Time

It has taken some time
to not see myself
as you saw me —

as someone easy to walk away from.

It has taken some time for me
to not want to walk away from me, too.

Not Sorry

Sometimes I think about
calling you up to say
I'm sorry
for wringing us out like a washcloth
and collecting all of these words
in a bucket
before dumping them out
for everyone to see.

But then I think,
they're a little bit beautiful.

But then I think,
we were a little bit beautiful.

And I am not sorry
that I found beauty
in the wreck you left my heart.

Ending

It is a coming home,
and it is a salvaging,
and it is a hope,
a hope for more.

I remind myself of this
on the days
it only feels like an ending.

No

No.
No, I was not happy.
Loving you was like
standing on an iceberg
getting smaller by the second,
and maybe sometimes
you would come
and stand beside me,
but even then,
it was cold,
and even then,
I was afraid
of how much water
surrounded us
on all four sides.
Loving you was like
sinking,
like
shrinking,
like
drowning.
No, I was not happy.

(But every now and then, you held my hand.)

(You don't do that anymore.)

Prey

I root for the mouse
to get away,
but that's not to say
I want the hawk to starve.
It's a matter of relating, you see.
I have been the thing
torn to shreds,
but I have never been
the thing that tears.
I have no talons,
I have never needed
to watch something smaller than me
bleed.
Did you need to,
(did you want to.)
What was it you were hungry for,
(what was it you were starving for.)

I am torn,
and I am bleeding,
but I guess
it wasn't
me.

Quiet

We are quiet,
but we are not out
of things to say.
I have turned the way you left
into poetry now
because nobody has ever told me
what to do with
all of these words
left in boxes
in my attic.
Collecting dust
and pounding on the ceiling.
So I write them
and we are
anything but quiet
in them,
do you hear us,
we are loud in them,
which is good because
we are not out
of things to say,
or perhaps I mean
that I am not.

I think maybe that you are.

I think maybe that's the saddest part of all.

Sometimes I Think

Sometimes I think my whole life
has been me pounding
on the insides of my windows,
waiting for someone to care enough
to stop and look inside.
Like I've gone missing
and I'm yelling, "I'm here, I'm here,"
but nobody knows to look for me,
everyone thinks it's just the wind, calling,
just the creaks in this old house, falling.
Sometimes someone pauses and I think,
this is it, this is it, this is it,
but they never look close enough
to see me.

Sometimes I think my whole life
has been me wanting
to be seen.

Sometimes I think my whole life
has been me clinging tight to the belief
that there's something here worth seeing.

This Heart of Mine

You always knew
what this heart of mine was,
and I think that's why
I can't believe
you didn't know
you were breaking it.

2016

That was the year I loved you,
I say,
and I say it like someone
who knows better now.
Me, I learn from my mistakes,
but you weren't a mistake,
I have called you many things,
many things,
but I have never called you a mistake.
(I have called you lost.)
(I have called you mine.)
If I know anything better now,
it's that other people have hands
that open just as easily as they close,
and somehow mine
only know how to close.
So I keep that in mind.
And I tell people
that was the year I loved you,
if they ask where I was,
what I was doing.
I tell people that was the year
I learned
that there are other people
for other people
and there is only

you

for me.

What's Best for Me

I hate that you think
you did
what's best for me.

I hate that you think
you have any idea
in all of the world
what's best for me.

But mostly I hate
that I can't get over
thinking you're
what's best for me.

Detonated

I call it folding
because it sounds
more elegant than
collapsing.
I stand tall
because my bones
and my pride
require it of me,
but inside,
I have been
detonated.
I pick through the rubble
but I can't find anything here
worth saving.
I guess that makes sense because
even before
you lit the fuse,
you couldn't find anything here

worth

saving.

I'm Convinced

I want you like
a child
wants to touch every fragile thing
up and down the aisles
of every store,
and I need you like
a wildflower
needs rain
in the middle of a drought,
and I'm convinced,
I'm convinced,
I love you like
nobody

has ever

loved anything

before.

Now I Wonder

He looks at me
the way you looked at me.

(I loved the way you looked at me.)

But now I wonder if it's only
how people look at me
when they know
    they're going
        to leave.

How Not To

If the question is
do I care,
the answer is
I am still trying
to learn from you
how not to.

Believe

There are things

we can't see

that we can only choose

to believe in,

and to me,

you are one of

those things.

A Thing That Goes

Sometimes I think that life
is much too short
and far too beautiful
to spend another moment
chasing after the things that go,
but then I think
our time together
was much too short
and far too beautiful
to let it be
a thing
that goes.

This

I think
it has always
been this:

you, looking
at the road,
at the mountains,
at the moon;

me,
only ever
looking
at you.

He Doesn't Realize

He asks me about you,
though he doesn't know it.
He thinks he's just asking
why I don't trust him,
why I won't let him in,
where my thoughts go
when I'm staring out the window.

He thinks he's just asking me to love him.

He doesn't realize
    he's also asking me
        to stop loving you.

I'm Sorry

I visit our grave twice a week,
I'm sorry,
twice a day,
I'm sorry,
I also sleep there every night.
I spend an hour smashing
the tombstone to bits
and another hour gluing
it back together.
I plant flowers and I let
the weeds grow wild
and strangle them.
I trace the letters of our names and mine
has deeper grooves than yours;
I trace the beginning and end dates and mine
ends on a different day than yours.

Our ghosts keeps me company,
so I am not alone.

We are laughing, and we are happy,
and I have never
                felt more
                              alone.

To Life

I want to love you to life,
I want to love you to life.

(But I cannot see you anymore.)

From the Sparrows

I decide each day
if I want to sit on this ledge
or dangle from it.
That's it, those are the options,
I cannot leave the ledge.
But I can sit
or I can dangle,
and I make that small choice
every morning.
It's better than nothing —
I used to only ever dangle.
I used to hang from my fingertips
while the crows called out my name.
Now some days I still dangle,
when I want to feel the strain of my muscles
and the pound of my heart,
but most days I climb up and sit
on this narrow little ledge
and I rest my head against the wall
and close my eyes and realize
that only some of the calls are from crows.

(The rest are coming from the sparrows.)

Unsure

I write everything
as though you're reading it,
but I'll write this
as though you're not—

I'm not sure I ever loved you,
but I'm just as unsure
if I'll ever
stop.

From the Beginning

I have loved you this long,
and precisely this long,
and just as long as this —

from the beginning.

(That's all there is.)

Pulse

There is no pulse on this page
until I put it there.
Each word is like the spike of an EKG,
like *live*,
like *live*,
like *please live*.

(I am desperate for a heartbeat.)

Are these words enough.

No,
how about these,
no,
how about these.

Are these something you might live for.

Are they something I might live for.

I hide my hands behind my back
because to others it's just ink,
but to me, but to me,
it's only ever blood from pages
I couldn't bring to life.

The Way That I Hold On

It is either my greatest weakness
or my greatest strength, this —

the way

that I

hold on.

My Heart Breaks Here

My heart breaks here,
that's all I know about here.

I draw an X on the map,
I try another town,
I try another town.

I never stay long,
just long enough to stare
at a new ceiling
in a new house,
just long enough to know
that there are cracks here, too.

So I draw another X.

I try another town.

(I try every town but yours.)

Because I already know
   my heart
      breaks there.

Nothing

You make me happy,
I'm sorry, I mean
you made me happy.
And I'm not worth the price
you paid for me now,
what price did you pay for me,
I know what price I paid for you.
My feet don't step right and
my eyes don't close right and
my skin doesn't fit right
is the price I paid for you.
A body that's mine,
that's only ever been mine,
and now it doesn't feel like it,
is the price I paid for you.
And that's to say nothing of my heart.
That's to say nothing of my heart,
let's say nothing of my heart,
I will say nothing of my heart,
because nothing
is now all
that it says.

Stolen

I loved our stolen moments,
until you started stealing

them

from me.

The Hardest Truths

Some of the hardest truths you will find are that

what you prioritize
will not always prioritize you

and

what you want
will not always want you

and

what you love
will not always love you

and

you have to decide
what you'll do with this.

March and You

In like a lion, out like a lamb,
they say about March
and I say about you.

In like "I want to be with you,"
out like "this is just too hard."

While I'm still standing here,
still standing here,

still roaring

at the top of

my lungs.

Anyway

She had flowers in her hair
and he had leaving in his shoes,
everybody knew it,
and deep down, she did too.

But she loved him anyway.

Which One of Us

I don't know which one of us broke it,

but I know which one of us decided

that it wasn't

worth

fixing.

Anyway, I Reach

I don't know if I reach because

my hands are empty

or if I reach because

I want you.

Anyway, I reach.

Fix It

The smallest of cracks
can splinter and spread and shatter
if you don't take the time to fix it.

And what I'm saying is,
I don't understand
why you won't take the time
to fix it.

Smaller

It took me a long time to learn

that just because

not everyone can hold me,

does not mean

I should ever make myself

smaller.

That's It

I had a dream that you remembered me.

That's it,
that's the whole poem.

Broken Glass

I have a fight in me,
and nothing civilized like
pistols at dawn, no,
more like a bar fight,
a brawl,
a couple of drunken fools
who think they know
a thing about a thing.
That's the kind of fight
I have in me,
yes, a dirty fight, an ugly fight,
I smash the bottle against the wall
and come at you with
the shards of it,
is how I tell you
not to go,
is how I growl at you
to stay,
I say, fight me, damn you, fight me,
no, I say fight for me, damn you, fight for me,
as your hands stay at your sides,
as you don't look me in the eye,
as you go quietly into the night
and everyone who walks past wonders
why I'm clinging to broken glass.

The Elephant in the Room

You may have buried the past,
but I dug it back up,
dusted it off,
framed it,
put it on the goddamn mantel.
It's the elephant in the room
I hang my coat on
and lean against when I'm tired.
Everyone knows better
than to ask me about it,
but I tell them about it anyways.
I say, oh that?
Let me tell you about that —

it is hard to be the one left behind.

(There isn't much else to tell.)

A Cure

I have scars on the wrong side
of my skin. I name them like
a warrior names his weapons.
That one is September 2nd and that
one is your smile and that one is
goodbye, I whisper just
loud enough for nobody
to hear, I shout just loud
enough for nobody
to hear because nobody
is anywhere close to near.
They used to bleed
the sick to try to cure them
of disease, and I think that if
you cut me open,
all that would spill out
is you. That is not to say
you are disease. It is just
to say that I carry you
within me. It is just to say
that I am hoping
there's
a cure.

All or Nothing

And I know I said all or nothing,

I know I said all or nothing,

but I cannot

stand

the nothing.

Stay

This whole time,
I've just been wishing
that you'd love me.

I should have wished
that loving me
would be enough to make you stay.

Miracles

There have been miracles, and

I think

that we

could be one.

Enough Things

I have watched

enough things end

to know

that I don't want this

to be one of those things.

Bravely

I do not love you fearlessly.

(I am afraid.)

And so I love you

bravely.

Ours

You took your dreams
with you when you left,
and you took my dreams
with you when you left,
and you left me

here with

ours.

Make Do

I'm not saying I adapt well,
but I adapt. I learn
how to sleep on a wet pillow. I dial
your number but I hang up
before it rings. I wish on airplanes,
on 11:12, on blades of grass if
I can't find a dandelion. I make do
with what I have, I make do with what
I don't have. Because what's the
alternative, no really, what's the alternative,
someone tell me, is there an alternative.

I am doing my best while I'm not
at my best, and I am proud of every
day that I wake up and make do in a world
that you're
not
in.

Looking for You

I am looking for you
under rocks.
I am lifting conversations
and touches and smiles,
looking for you.
I am staring at ceilings
that aren't mine,
looking for you.
I am saying Marco,
listening for Polo,
saying ready or not,
here I come,
looking for you.

I am saying I'm done
looking for you.

But when nobody is looking,
I
  always
        am.

~~Simply Impossible~~ Impossibly Simple

It is as simple as this:

all I want is you.

And it is as impossible as this:

all

I want

is you.

Regrets

I can tell you this about regrets:

whatever you think they weigh,

they

weigh

more.

Otherwise

When you asked if I was happy,
I thought you meant right here,
right now,
talking to you.

Otherwise,
the answer
would have been
no.

All the Same

I'm an open book of
I miss you,
a song turned all the way up to eleven of
I want you,
I scrub my face twice a day,
but it's still written all over it,
forehead to chin,
bold,
red,
dripping.

It says,
I know you are not looking, but

I love you

all

the same.

What Do You Give Up

You say you give up,
but what. What do you
give up, do you know exactly what
you're giving up, have you
thought about it, have you really
thought about it, do you know
that the thing you're
giving up is
me.

Say it,
not just
I give up.

Say,
      I give
            you up.

Eulogy

I'll be honest, some days this is
less poem, more eulogy. Do you
see it in the words, do you feel
the way I am waiting for you to say
I'm sorry for your loss
so I can say
there was nothing anyone could do.
Do you believe it when
I say it, do I say it like
I mean it.

Tell me, do I tell
a convincing lie.

I toss dirt down into
the grave, even though
the coffin's empty.

(There wasn't anything left to bury.)

Already Broken

The heart wants
what it wants, trust me,
I know. It's like a child
in the grocery store checkout line,
digging in its heels,
howling,
refusing to listen to reason,
refusing to relinquish its hold
on the thing that it wants,
needs,
has to have,
swearing it won't
break it.

I don't know how to tell it
that the thing it wants
is already
broken.

Flags

Dawn breaks, and so
do we. You keep waving
flags, and I cannot tell if
they're white or red, but
either way, it's time
for me to go. Past
time. Past tense. It was
time for me to go. It has been
time for me to go
for quite some time now, but,
you know, only one
of your hands
is holding any flags.

(The other is holding mine.)

Proud

Somebody once told me that
the strength is in never
letting them see how much they've
hurt you, but no, I think the strength
is in letting them see how much
you cared.

Instead of sheep I count the times
I put my heart out in the world,
small and bruised and fragile.

(I fall asleep proud.)

Origin Story

I was standing there,

holding heartbreak in my hands,

and I did not know what

to do with it.

(So I wrote it down.)

Now I See

I used to think that silence
was a knife you liked to shove
up in the space between my ribs,
but now I see that it's a shield
you hold up around yourself.

Now I see that you were never
trying to hurt me.

You were only trying

to save

yourself.

Endlessly Endlessly

I've been drinking about you,
oh no just sinking about you,
positively shrinking about you,
on-the-brinking about you,
pen-and-inking about you,
wondering-if-you-are-hoodwinking about you,
to be honest I guess
more than anything else
I am endlessly endlessly
thinking
about you.

Never Nobody

It's true, I cannot always see
the forest for the trees. But that means
when one falls, there is never nobody
there to hear it.

I tell them that I'm sorry,
I say, I know
it hurts
to fall.

But I will be your witness,
telling the world both
that you stood
and that you fell.

(And that you were beautiful.)

The Fool

I would always rather be

the fool who believed in you

than

the fool

who didn't.

Never Let It Be Said

Never let it be said

that I did not want you

badly enough.

In Here

I'm restless in here, screaming
in here, desperately, desperately reaching
in here, wanting in here, pleading in
here, hoping and hoping and hoping
in here, missing pieces in here, limbs
and bones gone in here, not breaking but
bending and bending in here, I'm
pacing in here, I'm waiting in here,
I'm yelling come back, come back
in here.

(Nobody can tell because still and still)

I'm smiling and
laughing and
living out there.

Too Soon

I am more afraid
of letting go too soon
than I am
of holding on too long.

Only the Beginning

Once upon a time,
I fell in love with a boy
who broke my heart.

I know it sounds
like an ending,
but I swear, I swear —

it was only the beginning.

Waiting

The song says waiting
is the hardest part, but no,
it would be so much harder
not to have something
worth waiting for.

This Heartbreak

This heartbreak is
light-years old, ancient,
scrawled upon cave walls
in fingerpaint or blood
somewhere time has never
touched it.

You know, I think
we all try to do better
than those that came before.

Heartbreak saw you go,
and thought —

not me, I think I'll stay.

Heavy

The world is heavy;
I have been trying for months
to lift it from where
it fell down at my feet.

And you keep saying
I am wrong, when what
you mean is that
you don't understand me.

Tell me, please tell me,
what is it like
to have somebody
love you
this much.

Jeopardy

Falling glass. A promise. My heart. (What is
broken.) The wind. The past. You.
(What is gone.) The radio. Your truck. Us.
(What is happiness.)

I'm sorry, you must answer in the correct tense.

(What was happiness.)

Tunnel

I have been in a tunnel
with no light at the end of it.

If now I am in one where
the light is very far away,
I still know
to be grateful
that there is any light at all.

Broken In

Not broken, no, not
broken. Now I say
broken in. Stretched, worn,
gives a little more. Gives and
gives and gives a little more.

(It isn't a bad thing.)

Between the Lines

Sometimes if I don't like what
the lines say, I try to read between
them. Like maybe every other
line says, "I don't mean what I'm
about to say," or maybe every
other line says, "I don't mean what
I just said." Like you're looking
at me with goodbyes sliding off
your tongue and I'm seeing a "for
now" you won't let fall.

Which is worse, false hope or
none.

I don't know how to hold on to
nothing, which is ironic because
that's all
I do.

Every Letter

What is poetry but
every letter I
am too afraid to send.

One Small Word

One small word, one
syllable, four letters,
and yet —

I have never held
anything bigger than
hope.

The Beginning

Unconditional means without
conditions. Not I love you
but. Not I love you despite, even
though, regardless of,
notwithstanding. I love
you and that is the end of it.

I love you and that
is the beginning of it.

I Can't Hear You

There is a hole in the middle of the living room
that neither of us talks about. We skirt the edges
of it, aware that it is dark down there, aware that
neither of us can see the bottom, aware that
we cannot live like this forever. There are nights
we come home blind drunk, and I think, how will
we not fall in, I think, how will this not be it. But
the morning comes, and we're back to having
breakfast with our backs against the wall, back to
pretending we didn't both lean over the sides of it
last night.

Sometimes I wonder if it would be so bad
to let it swallow us whole.

You stand on one side, and I stand
on the other, and I shout, "I love you,"
across the face of it.

And you lift your hand to your ear,
and mouth the words,
"I can't hear you."

Michelangelo

The backs of my eyelids
are painted like I'd imagine
the Sistine Chapel would be
if Michelangelo had been
in love with you, too.

Maybe I Was Wrong

I hold a pen, now,
instead of you, and I think —

maybe I was wrong about
what it will be that
saves me.

All I Have Left

I'm sorry I could not save them all. I have
carried what I could for some time now,
for such a long time now, but they
are heavy. I have had to drop some so that
I could keep moving. Some nights I reach
for them half-asleep and can't breathe for
missing them.

This is all I have left, this handful, this
small bunch I won't give up.

We drive through a light as it turns
yellow, and you look over at me
and smile.

(It's one of the ones I keep.)

Whiskey Drunk

Whiskey drunk and I don't miss you. Never
have. Never will. I take another shot and I
swear, I swear, I don't even remember your
name. Wine drunk and I've already called you
twelve times. Left a couple voicemails. Cried
my way through them both. Tequila drunk and
I found someone who looks enough like you
to pretend for the night, just for the night, to
dance and laugh and pretend for the night.
Beer drunk and the jukebox keeps playing
our song. (I keep playing it.) Still, I'm happy, I'm
happy, until I get home and you're not
there.

And the next morning when I
wake up with regrets, it is
no different than
any other morning.

I Still Look at You

I am soft, I don't think
you like that about me. In the
places the world should
have made me hard, I
still cry at movies and books
and love songs. My hands
still reach even after they've
been burned. I still look at you and
see sunrises and airplanes landing
and beginnings.

I still look at you and see the boy
I loved instead of the one who
broke my heart.

I still look at you.

A Someday

There is a someday
where you and I
are in the same place
at the same time, and
to think of it is like
a hand pressing firmly
against the small of my back —

it keeps me going.

A Reminder

You are a wound I touch
too often. If it ever even
thinks about closing, I jab
my finger inside of it and
wrench it back open. I like
to make it bleed. I like to feel
the warmth that lives
within it.

And it's nice to have a
reminder that it was real
for the days when you
pretend it wasn't.

Shouting Us

I can feel us trying
to become a whisper, so I
keep shouting us at the top
of my lungs, I keep howling
us, screaming us, echoing echoing
echoing us.

Because I have become
a memory before, and

I know how quickly they fade.

Nobody

I am nobody's love, and I stand where
nobody stands. If you look, you will see
nobody in my heart, nobody on my mind,
I wait and I wait and I wait for nobody.

Nobody makes me want more than this and
I long for nobody, I dream of nobody, I write
poetry for nobody.

And yet everyone thinks
I'm lying when
I tell them, to me, you are
nobody.

Anything But

Kiss me, I've been restless
over you. Kiss me, I've been
reckless over you. Kiss me,
I've been relentless over
you.

Kiss me, I've been

anything

but over you.

They Were Bright

I can't remember
which stars were above us
that night, but I remember
that they were
bright, and that I was
in love with you.

Silent Film

The world has gone silent and black and white, like a 1920s film, and the subtitles say someone is screaming. I thought I was on the train, but no, I'm tied to the tracks. I thought I was the villain, but no, I tied myself here. I thought the ropes must be tight, but no, I could get up, I could go. The train bears down, and I thought I would save myself, but no —

the subtitles say someone is screaming.

But my mouth is open, and

nothing

is coming

out.

Two Settings

My two hands have two
settings: hold on for dear
life or let go. And they
get them confused, they
let go when I dangle
from the edge of a cliff and
they hold on for dear life
to you.

The end result is the same.

This Poem

I traded you for
this poem, and you know —

if these words don't love me
any more than you did,
at least they don't love me
less.

The Nerve

We fell apart slowly at first —
one card fluttering away on
the breeze. But we hardly
noticed (there were so many
others) so we let it go. We let it
go, and then we let the next one
go, and the next one, and the
next one. And when suddenly
there was no roof and suddenly
there were no walls and suddenly
there was no us — we had
the nerve, the nerve, the goddamn
nerve to wonder where it all
went wrong.

Frozen

My hands need gloves,
but my heart can take the cold.

(It's been through this before.)

I'm not sure which is frozen,
time or me, but something
isn't moving, and I know it isn't
you.

I try not to take it personally, I
remind myself every day:

you are moving toward your dreams.

It only feels like away to me.

High School Math

It's like a problem from high school
math, though those I could usually solve:

if you are at point A, moving farther and
farther away, and I am at point B, standing
perfectly still as a tree, how long will it take until
I don't love you anymore.

Metaphors

He says I hide behind
metaphors, but I say it is
not so much hiding as it is
wanting badly to be found.

Burning Bridges

I will tell you
that if I decide
to set this bridge on fire,
it will not be
to prevent you
from crossing after me.

It will only be
to prevent me
from crossing after you.

(Again and again and again.)

Firsts

I don't remember my first words or
the first steps I took. I don't remember
the first time I ran through rain or the
first time I fell back and made a snow
angel. I don't remember, of course
I don't remember, the first time I cried,
the first time I laughed, the first time
I lost something and couldn't find it
again, the first time I learned that
not everything that goes comes back.

But I remember the first time I saw you, and that
it was the first time I let go of my heart.

Even knowing it might not come back.

Memories

I don't

hold onto

memories

so much

as they

hold onto

me.

Devastation

I have met devastation, yes,
passed him in a hallway once, got
a good look at him, invited him
to stay the night, but by the morning,
he was gone. I thought that might be it, but
we crossed paths again a little while later, and
this time, we spent some months side by
side, sleeping in the same bed, though
he didn't make it feel less empty. He didn't
say anything when I cried, never tried
to hold my hand, but he also made it clear
he didn't want to leave. He made a game of
whispering your name in my ear, you know,
middle of the night, middle of the day, any time
I started to forget he was there.

Maybe you've met him, another time, another
place, but I know I never introduced you.

He was never here when you were.

Where You Are

It is November where you
are, at least. I don't know if
it's cold or if they call it
autumn there, but it is
November where you are,
at least. Things are
contemplating hibernation
here, things like bears and
bats and bees, but I
have never been more
awake. I and hope. And
hope. And hope. It is
November where you are,
at least.

And the moon is the moon and
the sky is the sky and I love you there
the same as I loved you here.

Tumbleweed

I learned today that
a tumbleweed is
the part of a certain kind of
plant that breaks away
from its roots.

It just has to go; the wind
is calling and it has to go.

(I think you understand.)

A Home

I have built a home here—
your words, the brick;
my hopes, the mortar.

It will stand or it will fall.

But for now, the rain can't touch me.

Wreckage

We are down to this: wreckage
only sometimes washing up
onto shore.

The seas are largely calm.

Nothing has raged here in some time.

But then I hear your name.

(Wreckage.)

Ruins

If I had to describe
myself in just one
word, it would be

ruins.

(Noun or verb?)

Both.

How Much

You asked a question, I have
an answer—

yes, I knew what I was risking.

I was just wrong about
how much.

A Broken Thing

Have you ever tried
to wrench open a car door
after an accident?

So you know how hard it is
to open a broken thing.

Binary Stars

If you were here, I would lie beside you
and tell you about binary stars. I would point to
Sirius A, dancing with Sirius B, bound by a push
and a pull and a storm. I would say, Sirius A, it shines
so bright, hardly anyone sees Sirius B. I would say,
you know, once, Sirius B was the brighter of the
two. I would say, you know, once, Sirius B was
brighter than the sun.

But it burned too brightly, it burned itself out, and
now we can't see it anymore. It's dying, now, half
alive, now, it's only a matter of time.

Everyone points out Sirius A, how beautifully it
lights up the night sky.

But when I see it, all I can think is that
somewhere beside it, Sirius B

is dying.

A Moat

It has never been just an
ocean, any more than the
moon is just a rock, any more than
the sun is just a star, any more than
I am just in love with you.

When is a body of water a moat?

When everything you want is on the other side of it.

For You

This is a poem that I
don't want to write. I will
probably call it something like
For You, and it won't rhyme.
I will be both sorry and glad
when other people tell me
they relate to it. I will hope that
you read it. I will hope that you
don't read it. I will try to find a
way to sneak in the words *I
love you*, maybe the words
I miss you, probably the words
come back. It will be hard to call it
poetry. I will reread it half a dozen
times, but it will never become just
words, just letters, just a piece of paper.

It will always be something like
bravery, something like my heart.

It will always be for you.

Looking

Maybe I've been doing this
all wrong, looking for you instead
of looking for love.

So now I look for love.

(I still hope to find you.)

A Sign

I ask the universe for
a sign as though
the fact that you're not here

isn't

one.

Mistaken

I'm sorry, I've mistaken you
for somebody else, I say, to
strangers on the street I
chase after when they have
your laugh and to you
when you tell me
you don't love me anymore.

To Feel Alive

Some people need to
jump out of planes
to feel alive; I just need
to love you.

Two Months

I keep running around
the kitchen island, and you
keep chasing me, and we
are laughing, and
I never let you catch me, I
never let you catch me, because
if I do, two months will pass and
you won't love me anymore.

Maybe Mars

Maybe Mars just had its heart broken.
We declare no sign of life, and we do not
hear it say, *I'm trying, I'm trying.* We say it's
cold up there, it's dark up there, and we do not
hear it say, *I didn't use to be this way.* We look around
a bit and go, and we do not
hear it say,

please don't leave me here alone.

Wide as the World

I am trying to open my
arms as wide as the world
because I don't know which
part of it you might be in
or if you might need me.

Less

I saw a movie today, and for
the first time in a long time,
my hand did not feel empty
without yours in it. I do not
think I'd call that loving you
less; I think I'd call that
starting to forgive you
for loving me less.

To the Light

I follow my heart
through the darkness
because I trust
it is leading me
to the light.

Life Lessons

You cannot pour love into a cup
that they have covered with
their hand.

You can try, I mean,
you can try.

But it will leave a mess and you

will have to mop it up

alone.

It's Complicated

When people ask about us I say
it's complicated, but maybe it isn't.

Maybe I just love you and maybe you

just don't care.

Not Enough

I like to think that
Wendy went off and
built herself a life,
a good life.

And that Peter missed her.

(Just not enough.)

A Hollow Victory

I am soft-edged but sharp-
tongued. *I love you* is a challenge
I handed you, and you did not
know how to meet it. It is a hollow
victory that years later still tastes
strongly of defeat.

You have never asked for my
forgiveness, but here, take it,
I don't want it anymore. Put it with
I love you.

Either where you put
the things you care about or
where you put the things you

don't.

The Ocean's Memory

If water has a memory, I wonder if
the ocean thinks we're still
together.

It would only remember us laughing.

It never saw me cry.

Too Much

Maybe this is enough
hurt. You know? Maybe this is
too much hurt
to still be able to call it

love.

Say It's the Sea

The tide grabs you by
the ankles and drags you
back out to sea every time
you reach for me. Right? Say
it's the tide. Say it's the sea.
Say you are not
choosing this.

Be Brave

What I know of fear
is that it has cost me
far more
than bravery ever has.

Maybe Someday

Maybe someday
this will all
make sense,
but for now
I still love you
too much
to understand.

Darker

They say the night is always
darkest before the dawn, so
each night, I wait for the
dawn, only to discover that

it can get

darker.

One of Them

I imagined whole lives
for us, I imagined whole
lives for us.

Yes, this was one of them.

It wasn't the one I hoped for.

On Both of Us

Fool me once, shame on you,
fool me twice, shame on me,
no, you know what—

shame on both of us.

With Patience

Sometimes I fight
for you with patience,
and oh, you should know,
it is the heaviest
weapon
I wield.

In This One

In this one, I love you like gunpowder. It isn't anything without a spark, and so it isn't anything. In this one, we are no good for each other. We are wounds that never graduate to scars because we can't stop picking at them. In this one, everyone tells me to let go. They don't see how far the drop is. In this one, you stop calling and you never tell me why.

In this one, I don't miss you.

(In this one, it turns out, I lie.)

It Thinks It

My brain is sorry when it gently
takes the reins back from my
heart. It is sorry, and it does not
say I told you so.

But it thinks it.

I Hope, I Hope, I Hope

My name is common enough that
you must hear it from time to
time, and oh, I hope, I hope, I
hope, each time, it breaks

your little

heart.

This Is Not Benevolence

What can I do with this love. I throw
fistfuls out my window like a princess
in a parade but this is not benevolence
no this is not benevolence this is
desperation. Please take it please take
it away far away please take it far away.
I have so much and he does not want
it and it is rotting here inside of me. Gather
it in your arms and make a bouquet for him
or her tonight. Take it home take it away give
it to someone who'll want it treasure it
keep it give it to someone who'll keep it.

I have so much and he does not want it.

I am so much and he does not want me.

Hard to Love

You think you are

hard to love, but,

in my experience,

you are hard

to stop loving.

Howl

I thought it would be easier
once everyone stopped asking
about you, but now all I want to
do is pull out my chair and stand
up on it and howl your name

at the top of

my lungs.

The Sky

The sky is falling and I
love you. There is plaster
in my hair and I love you.
Stars on my cheeks and I
love you. Clouds in my lungs
and I love you. Airplanes
in my eyes and I love you.
Birds in my ears and I love
you. The moon in my hands
and I love you. The sun on my
tongue and I love you.

The world stops turning but
you spin me and above us
I see something we will
someday call
the sky.

Fiction

You know, I could pick up my pen and
write you still in love with me.

But it would hurt to have to call it fiction.

Yours

Just because
you break something
doesn't mean it isn't

still

yours.

Pieces

Two is made up of two ones,
but what is one made up of?

No, I know, pieces.

So many, so many
pieces.

Maybe I'm Wrong

The birds are all singing, and they're
singing like they don't know. Probably
they don't. Probably their little pounding
hearts beneath their little fluttering wings
could not handle the knowing.

Or maybe I'm wrong, it could be
I'm wrong.

Maybe they know and they

sing anyway.

Catch Me

They say that timing's a bitch, and
maybe they're right. Maybe I will always
love you too much in all the wrong
moments, and maybe you will never
love me enough in all the right ones.
Maybe I will always turn to look at
you just after you've turned away.
We made a game of it, in your truck,
seeing who could catch the other
looking, and

I am looking.

I am looking.

Catch me, I am looking.

An Ocean

I am falling
out of love
with you, I am.

It just takes
some time
to drain
an ocean.

That Was Me

I'm sorry, I know
you never asked
to be loved this much.

No, I forgot,
that was

me.

Eighth Wonder

Sometimes you'd look at me like
I was the eighth wonder of the
world, and all I wanted
was to be somewhere
you wouldn't leave.

No Hitch, No Falter

It's getting easier every day
not to be with you.

Did you hear that?

No hitch, no falter, you
couldn't even tell it was
a lie.

(I learned from the best.)

The Least

I'm afraid that this
will be the least I ever
love you.

Mercy

They tell me to
set fire
to everything
he ever
touched.

And in my chest,
my heart begs for
mercy.

I Live Around It

I've never stopped loving
anyone I've really loved
before; they just leave and I
live around it.

Apart

I thought nothing
could keep us
apart.

And if something
did, I didn't think
it would be you.

The Kindest Thing

The kindest thing
you could ever give me
is answers.

I guess the kindest thing
I could ever give you
is to try to understand
without them.

Grasping

Sometimes I'm looking and I can't
find the right words to tell you I'm
lost without you. It's like grasping
at thin air for something that might
have a chance of saving you. All
the words I think might be the right
ones are just out of reach, just
across the country, just over the
ocean, just possibly in the part
of my heart you still have.

I wish you were here.

I would say it better if you were.

Liars

I keep dreaming
that you come back
and say you're sorry
and I say it's okay.

I keep dreaming
that we're both liars.

Sad Little Poems

I could write sonnets
to the way that
I love you.

But instead I write
these sad little poems
to the way that
you don't care.

All for Me

I want you to know, there was a
time my heart beat more for you
than it did for me.

Two beats for every one,
six for every three.

It's quieter now.

But when it beats,
it's all for me.

Magic Trick

I keep looking in
the same empty box
for love, like

it's a magic trick, like

—*abracadabra*—

he loves me now.

Tsunami

If anything, you
are a tsunami
beneath my bridge.

Tell Me

Tell me, what kind of
fairy tale ends with
and then he never came back.

(The kind that isn't about him.)

Pretenders

I still love you even though I don't call it that
anymore. Self-preservation has its own
dictionary and I highlight words like *gone*
and words like *better off*, reread them
every night before bed. On the palm of
one hand, I write *you love the idea of
him, not him.* On the palm of the other,
I write *you love who you thought he could
be, not him.* In the shower I scrub hard
at every word between *love* and *him*.

This is what love makes of us:

it makes us pretenders.

You pretended you loved, and now
I pretend I
don't.

It Doesn't Have to Be

You say it is

what it is,

but oh,

it doesn't

have

to be.

Make a Liar of Me

Like Kevin McCallister standing outside
screaming, "I'm not afraid anymore!"
until the man with the snow shovel
appears and makes a liar of him—

I stand and scream,
"I don't love him anymore!"

But I know if you appeared,
you'd make a liar of me.

Nothing to Be Proud Of

We took a taxi to the finish line
of a marathon and thought that it
would count.

And I said I loved you because
I thought someday I would.

And you said you'd stay because
you hoped someday you could.

They gave us our medals, but
we don't hang them on our wall.

There is nothing to be proud of here.

A Thousand Love Poems in a Trench Coat

I didn't hang the moon for
you, but I could have. I would
have. I can't look at a Monet
without pointing out an errant
brush stroke, but I've been looking
at you for months and I can't find
a goddamn thing wrong. You are
so strong and sure and I am a
thousand love poems in a trench
coat trying not to fall apart.

You are a reason, a home; a hope,
a song; a promise a promise a
promise and I

am not so special, I just
love you.

Imagine

Imagine you love me. Close your eyes and imagine you love me. Imagine I am breaking you. Imagine I have your heart in my hands and I am breaking you. Imagine you leave. Imagine I push you so hard that you leave. Imagine I say I'm sorry. Imagine I call just when you're moving on and I say I'm sorry. Imagine you love me again. Close your eyes and imagine you love me again you love me again you love me again.

Imagine I am breaking you.

Imagine *I*

am breaking

you.

The Rest of Me

I say I'm sorry to
everyone who loved me
after you.

They only got
the rest of me.

This and Not That

This just like that? No, this is not just like that. I don't write about that, I don't think about that, I don't wake up in the middle of the night reaching for that. This is better than that, this is sweeter than that, this is ten miles higher and deeper than that. This is centuries from that, this is light years from that, this is a hop and a skip and a plane ride from that. This is all and not all of the nothing of that, this is here unlike that, this is real unlike that, this is happiness, ever so clearly not that, this is—

this and not that.

This is not just like that.

This is love and I know now

that has never been that.

House on Fire

This is still how I want to be loved: strong
arms, strong heart, certainly, with certainty.
This is still how I want to be loved: like even
on the days we are a house on fire, I am the
thing you'd run back in for. This is still how I
want to be loved: earthquake shaken and car
alarm loud. This is still how I want to be loved:
like I am the reward and not the cost.
This is still how I want to be loved:

by you.

By nobody but

you.

Shadow

I thought I left my shadow back
where you still love me, and that she
is holding your hand, and she is
laughing, and she is telling you
her favorite stories and you are
telling her yours, and I thought
that sounded beautiful.

But it turns out I am the shadow.

I am not holding your hand and I
am not laughing.

We are out of stories and none
of this is beautiful.

I am just not here.

I am just not here.

2023

In 2023, there will be a hurricane with his name on it, and I'm telling you right now, it will make a mess of things. When they tell you to board your windows, do not open them instead. When they tell you to stay inland, do not go down to the beach to meet it. And oh, when they tell you to be ready to pack up your things and go—

(when they tell you to be ready to pack up your things and go—)

do not build a home inside of it.

do not build a life inside of it.

do not, do not—whatever you do, do not—

lose yourself

inside of it.

Cracks

I put a cup over this love and
slide a piece of paper under it.

I don't want to kill it, it just
scares me.

I take it outside to set it free, but
there are cracks in this house.

It keeps finding its way back
inside.

The Last Thing

My hand is tired of holding this pen and
waiting for the rest of the words to come. The ink
is long-dry, I'm sure, but I can't put it down
without making a lie of the last thing
you said to me.

You know, I can forgive you not
coming back. But I can't forgive you

promising

you would.

All the Brighter

Who I'm going to be is miles away from
who I was going to be. You weren't just
a detour, just a scenic route, just the
pull of a train switch. No, you were a
different train entirely. I got off the one
I was on and got on yours, and it took
me someplace beautiful, left me
someplace dark. I am finding the
light, though. I am finding the light
and it is

all the brighter

because I've seen

the dark.

Bloom

Don't write me off yet; beneath
these dead & dying leaves is
something that still knows how

to bloom.

Lightning in a Bottle

We caught lightning in a
bottle and watched it
flash and crackle like
our own private sky,
'til one day you freed
it when I wasn't looking.

Maybe I was the only
one who saw it as
something beautiful.

Maybe all you ever saw
was something that was

trapped.

Eyes Wide Open

Someone fleeced me of a year's worth
of faith once so now I don't carry much
on me. No, I keep my pockets light, just
the bare minimum needed to get through
the day tucked in them. I don't spend it
on weather forecasts. I don't spend it on
train schedules. I don't spend it on men
with vagabond smiles and heretic hearts.

You know the saying, *he robbed me blind?*

He robbed me

eyes

wide open.

The Dark

Every morning I send the moon off
to find you. I say he is the one with
going in his boots and my heart in
his hands. I say you'll know him by
his laugh. The sun keeps me company
while I wait and I want to curse him
for shining so brightly but I know
he's only trying to help. When the
moon comes back she is sorry, she
is always sorry. She says you are
somewhere not even the stars can
find you.

She says she'll try again tomorrow.

But for tonight I look to the sky, afraid

you will never be free of the dark.

Whatever It Takes

I said
whatever it takes,
but I didn't know
it would take
this much.

Better Now

I am never going to call
that love again. Not
because I'm bitter, but—

because I know better now.

My Some

There is no good in this, or should I say,
I have not found it. It took three years, but
all this rain has finally washed you free of
your rose-colored paint. (What's underneath
is not worth keeping.) You know, I was so
proud of myself for giving you my all but I
see now you only wanted my some. If
given the chance to see myself through
your eyes, I would not take it.

I know what I am, and
it will never be
what your absence tried
to make me.

Not That Far

I kept moving the line for
you so that you won't have
crossed it, but I can't move it
that far.

The Ones That Stay

I am not much for
shooting stars;

I prefer the ones that

stay.

You Could

I used to think, if you could
only see the way I love you,
if you could only hear the
way I miss you, if you could
only feel the way I want you,
surely you would stay.

But then I realized

that you could—

and you are choosing not to.

Now I Am

Now I am goodbye. You hear that? Now
I am indifference, now I am not looking
back, now I am making decisions for the
both of us. Now I am running, callousness,
cowardice. Now I am covering my ears
and closing my eyes and singing *la la la*
at the top of my lungs over the sound of
you calling my name. Now I am done,
I am done, I don't care what you are I am
done. Now I am gone, I am gone, I don't care
that you need me I am gone. Now I am
goodbye. You hear that? Now *I* am.

Did this feel good to you?

Because it feels
terrible
to me.

For a Long Time

For a long time I blamed timing. Cursed the clocks for getting it all wrong, running too slow, running too fast, I don't know just getting it all wrong. For a long time I blamed the universe. Thought there must be one star that didn't get the memo to line up with the rest, got lost on its way, let its mind wander, I don't know just didn't line up. For a long time I blamed myself. Figured I pushed you too hard, wanted you too much, held on too tightly, I don't know just ruined the whole thing. But now—

I blame you.

For saying it was timing, for saying
it was the universe.

For saying it was

me.

Kamikaze Love

Some of me went to war for you. I know you want
me to say all but I won't lie to you my fear stayed
home couldn't convince self-preservation to come
along left caution on the bedside table. I flew into the
heart of battle without an exit plan they call that
kamikaze I loved you like kamikaze love like I didn't
plan on leaving it alive. I planned on loving you all the
way to the grave I did instead I loved you half a year
maybe more turns out it's not much of a war once the
other side surrenders. Maybe I should just be glad I
made it home in one piece it still counts as one piece
even if you're riddled with holes so maybe I should
just be glad.

Back home with my fear and my self-preservation
and my caution waiting

for one of them to keep me warm.

Here's to the Nights

Here's to the nights
you said you loved me.

They're gone now, but I
still drink to them.

Lost is Lost

Someone told me once that they'd rather
get lost in space where they could see
the stars than in the bottom of the ocean
where it's just dark.

But I know from loving you that
lost is lost.

Even if it's beautiful.

What a Waste

You draw your lines with invisible ink so I never know when I'm crossing one. (You tell me afterward with silence.) Our love is a forest you've rigged with tripwires and bear traps, and I do not go slowly through it. I do not tiptoe, and I am not cautious. I leave pieces of myself behind, like an offering, but the deeper I go, the more dangerous it gets. It is dark and I don't know where I am. It is dark and I don't know who I am. It is dark and I know that I love you.

When the first match lights, I think to myself, *what a waste, what a waste.*

And as it all burns down around me, I marvel at how the match comes away unscathed.

And the Phoenix Said

When it was over they pulled
the phoenix from the sky by
its burning hot tail feathers and
asked how it felt to die.

And the phoenix said, *all I
remember is leaving his arms.*

They asked if it was worth it.

And the phoenix said, *I had
to try it.*

They asked if it hurt to be reborn.

And the phoenix said, *mostly it hurt
to be reborn
as something that
still loves him.*

How Much More

When I donate blood, I don't ask how much they'll take from me, I just assume that they'll take what they need. I trust that they'll leave me enough to survive, that they won't take too much, but I wonder at what point I'd stop them. If I would stop them. How light-headed would I need to be? How weak-kneed, how dizzy, how brave, yes, brave, I would need to be brave. To stop someone taking. To say, *I have no more to give.* To walk away from someone who says they need more.

I would need to be brave, but how brave.

How brave. How brave. Oh god how much more

brave.

Come and Get It

Forgiveness sits on a table
in my foyer. It's yours if you
want it, but you have to come
and get it.

In This House

There is a wooden sign hanging in the foyer that says, "In this house, we choose love," and sometimes I catch myself staring at it and thinking—in this house, we don't know how to hold hands without our fingernails breaking skin; in this house, we don't know how to kiss without biting down; in this house, we don't know how to say *goodbye* without adding a *good riddance*; in this house, we slip lies into one another's pockets and keep secrets in our own; in this house, we swallow bandages and glue and leave the wounds wide open; in this house, I am standing in the foyer, and you're a thousand miles away.

Because in this house, we wanted to choose love, I swear to God we wanted to.

But in this house, we forgot to.

From Afar

I've always been one
for hand-to-hand combat,
while you shoot arrows
from afar.

Either way, it hurts, but—

you don't have to see my face
when the arrow lands.

Memorized

You took a highlighter to
my loneliness.

Don't worry, I
have it memorized now.

Unless

I know what I want, I want a mile, not an inch* / a flower, not a petal* / a feast, not a crumb* / a torch, not a match* / a lifetime, not a night* / a forest, not a twig* / a star, not a firefly* / a diamond, not a rock* / an ocean, not a puddle* / a novel, not a word* / a storm, not a drizzle* / a shout, not a whisper*.

(unless that's all you have to give.)

Grenade

You slipped a grenade inside
my mouth when you kissed me
goodbye and walked away with
the pin between your teeth.

(There is nothing here to come back to.)

About You

That I was wrong to trust you
says more about you
than it does
about me.

Wrong

It's like a test question where
you got the right answer but
you didn't get to it the right way.

Yes, if you wanted to leave, it was
for the best you left.

But the way you went—

it makes the whole thing wrong.

You Won't Know This

You won't know this, but I kissed your dog's head on the way out. I ran my fingertips along the frame of the painting in the hallway. I folded the blanket on the couch. I put the book I borrowed back on the bookcase in the living room. I hung my key on the peg by the door. I sat on the front stoop for a minute, for two. I sat in my car for another minute, for two. I sat at that first stop sign for another minute, for two.

You won't know this, but I cried. You might not care to know it, but I tried.

To leave you with more than a book, a key, a dog staring out the window after me.

To leave you with more than a note taped to your bedside wall.

(To not leave you at all.)

Still Always

I am still always the girl who snuck downstairs at midnight the year she found out Santa wasn't real, just in case. I left out milk and cookies one more time, just in case. I checked all of the presents beneath the tree for his name the next morning, just in case. It didn't matter that I'd been told backward and forward the truth of things. It didn't matter that it never made that much sense believing in him in the first place.

I am still always that girl.

I believe and I believe until I can't anymore, and—

I'm sorry. I can't anymore.

What It Was

It was what it was to me.

And that doesn't change

no matter what it was

(or wasn't)

to you.

Love and Hurt

It was love first, I know that it was love first. But then for a while in the middle there it was some combination of love and hurt, maybe 90/10, just 90/10, manageable at 90/10, still manageable at 80/20, survivable at 70/30, a little harder at 60/40, and then 50/50, 50/50 was bad, 50/50 was rough, not knowing on any given day which half of me would say enough was enough, and that's to say nothing of now, now, now when the hurt takes up more space than the love.

Now when I'm not sure
there's still any love at all.

Still On It

I understand that you needed
to burn
the bridge.

But did you need to burn it
with me
still on it?

Whether or Not

I would bend over backward for you. I would. I would jump through hoops, I would run a mile in heels, I would keep the windows open in the middle of a thunderstorm because I never want you to not have a way out of the rain. I would give you the very best part of me, the thing at the center that makes me who I am, the thing that bleeds too much and scars too easily and knows both of these things but still pulses, but still wants, but still wants you, I would give it to you. I would let you walk away with it over and over again. Not because I'm a fool and not because I don't know better but because the only thing I do know better is that I was meant to love you.

Whether or not
you were meant to love me.

A Thing That Happened

You said you'd always
care about what
happens to me,

but I don't think you realize

that you
are a thing
that happened to me.

No Easier

You know,
knowing I had to do it
didn't make it any easier
to have to do it.

What We Are Now

I think the hardest part is
that we can't have been
what I thought we were
if this is what
we are now.

A Problem

I used to only want the kind
of love I could not live without,
but now I can see
where that might be
a problem.

Can't Be Sure

I don't bleed heartbreak anymore.

But then again, nobody
cuts me open anymore.

So I guess

I can't

be sure.

The Hard Way

Someday,
you will be nothing more
than a lesson learned the hard way.

But for now,
I still have not learned it.

At the Bottom of the Sea

People act like I docked my boat
after you and just haven't been
brave enough to sail again.

They don't know
that it's at the bottom of the sea.

They don't know
that I'm down there with it.

The Hardest Part

The nights are hard, but they're not the hardest. Nor is the winter, the snow, that bone-deep cold. Not crowds, not when I'm alone. Memories, not even memories, they hurt but they're not the hardest. Not someone else with your name, not someone else with your laugh, not someone else, not just the simple fact of someone else. Not sunrises, not sunsets. There are dreams that are hard to wake from, sure, but they're still not the hardest part.

The hardest part is the hope.

The hardest part

is the goddamn

hope.

Still There

I still love you, I just
don't tell you anymore.

You can dam a river but
the water's

still

there.

Sadness

I give sadness a hard time, but at least

it never

leaves me.

I Still Believe

People seem surprised
that I still believe in love,

but it's not love's fault
you didn't want it

any more than it's my fault
you didn't want

me.

The Why

To be clear, you are still the who.
I just have no idea about the where.
The when. The how.

The why.

All or None

I cry more easily now. Happy, sad, it doesn't
matter, I cry more easily now. Missing you is a
program inside of me that never stops running,
takes up bandwidth, bogs down my memory. I
keep it minimized most of the time. I do other
things. I know it's there, but look, this is how far
I've come, I can do other things. Even laugh,
even love, even love someone else. Even try to, I
mean, even want to. Even really believe that
it's time to.

The trouble is, I'm an all or none of a girl.

And once you give your all away,
all that's left to give is
your none.

Waiting

I am not tired of waiting,
but I am tired of not knowing
what I'm waiting for.

A Mess

Love does not go quietly. I drag it out screaming, holding onto anything it can on its way to the door, like that text where he says that he misses me or that look in his eyes when he asks how I've been. Love howls, digs in its heels and its nails, doesn't get a chance to pack so leaves behind hope, leaves behind want, leaves behind memories.

I can tell you this, love is not getting its security deposit back.

Because love made
a mess of
this place.

How Long

I've never let a dream die before. Never
put it in the attic, closed the door, and let
it starve. I don't know how long it takes, does
anyone know how long it takes.

No, I know, you killed yours differently.

You drove it to the airport and told it

you didn't love it anymore.

Unfinished Business

I've been accusing you of haunting me, and
I'm just writing to say I'm sorry. I'm sorry.
You're not the ghost, I am. Shouting and
you can't hear me. Right in front of you
and you can't see me. This isn't living.
What is this, this isn't living. There's a
bright light at the end of this hallway and
someone said it offers peace, but you're
not there so I'll stay here. I'll stay here.

I'm not sure if my unfinished business is
unloving you or being loved by you.

Either way, I'll never be free of you.

Either way, you'll never be free
of me.

When They Ask Me

When they ask me what happened, I tell them all the things you told me. I say timing, I say distance. I say circumstances, I say it was just too hard. I say it isn't that we don't care about each other, no, it isn't that we don't care about each other.

I tell them all the things you told me.

But in my mind I say,
he didn't think we were worth it.

In my mind I say,
he didn't think I was worth it.

And to Think

And to think,
I called
that love.

Solar Flare

I still love you sometimes. Sometimes,
just sometimes. It's not sunshine
anymore, more like a solar flare.

When it fades, I remember.

Or maybe—

it fades when I

remember.

Something That Can Leave You

The trouble is, it stops being a dream
once it comes true.

It becomes something that
can leave you.

What Would You Do

I would never tattoo someone's name on me, but I would tattoo your thumbprint on the curve of my hip. I would tattoo your lifeline across the palm of my own hand. I would tattoo your constellation two inches south of my collarbone where I could hand-to-heart wish on it on every exhale, when all of the stars fall.

What would you do if you knew
there was no chance you would ever
regret it?

I would love you.

I would love you.

Instead of Peace

Love is a fight I've been picking with you for years now. You sharpen your sword against the way I cling to you in my sleep, and I wake up with surrenders in my mouth. I spit them in the sink before I kiss you. Nobody said this would be easy, and it isn't. It won't be.

But you could aim for my heart, and you don't.

And I could aim for your head, but I won't.

Instead of *I love yous* we exchange *do you still love mes*.

Instead of peace you bring me

joy.

So I Walk

My heart brakes. That is not a typo, it slams its
foot down on the pedal so hard I fly through the
windshield. I am more bruise than love now, more
splintered glass than want now. By the time I get back
up again, you have taken the key from the ignition.
The key you put in there, the first one to ever fit, the
first one to ever start it. You throw it in the reeds,
somewhere neither of us can find it. You don't look,
but I do, though it gets harder and harder to want to.

So I walk. I walk, no heart to drive me.

I walk, no love to
guide me.

So Much Space

You took up so much space in my heart, and I haven't rearranged it since you. Everything else is still pushed up against the walls. Someone said I should use this space to dance, but there is no music in here, just echoes of the things we meant to say softly, the things we never meant to say at all, the things I thought I would have a chance to say later. Was my heart always this big? It feels bigger now, emptied of you. Later I think this will be a good thing.

But for now, it is drafty in here.

For now, I hate every inch of the space
that wasn't enough
to hold you.

Forgive Me

Forgive me, I keep thinking about how many horses died at war. They never asked to be there. Did they even know that they were being led to battle. Did they even know that they could rebel and turn and run. Forgive me, I keep thinking about the way things shouldn't be. It doesn't matter that they are, they shouldn't be, and that keeps me up most nights. Forgive me, I keep thinking about whether I would know the difference between a sunrise and a sunset if I did not know the time. Can I tell a beginning from an ending. Would one bring hope and one bring sadness or would I see beauty in them both.

Forgive me, I keep thinking about you.

You always knew that you could run.

Maybe I Was Right

The world didn't end. Isn't that something?
Nobody holding my hand and still I stand. Isn't
that something? We are such brittle, boneless
things, always fighting for what we want and
never what we have. This isn't something. This
isn't something.

This is you saying the universe is chaos.

This is me saying the universe is for us.

In the middle of the night, you said
that maybe I was right.

This is a memory you don't have anymore.

This is a memory I don't want anymore.

So Long

I don't regret asking the question.

But I do regret spending so long
thinking you're the answer.

The Audacity of Heartbreak

I am here to speak to the audacity. The audacity!
The audacity of love, for starters. The sheer
audacity of love, which is to say nothing of
the audacity of heartbreak, let us say nothing
of the audacity of heartbreak. Oh no, and the
audacity of dreams? The absolute audacity of
dreams! And of course the audacity of beauty—
moreover, the audacity of sunrises. The audacity
of the ocean, such a thing, the unfathomable
audacity of the ocean. And can you even
comprehend the audacity of the moon? Of
the stars? Of the blue of the night sky? I
cannot, I tell you, I can absolutely not, but
nonetheless I find myself before the audacity
of joy. Of happiness? Yes, I suppose it falls to
me to speak to the audacity of happiness

and how I was in love once (the audacity of love)
beneath the silver moon (the audacity of the moon)
and held your hand in mine (the audacity

of heartbreak.)

If Given the Chance

How do you get over the things you are still buried beneath? The things you'd call regrets if you weren't sure you'd do them all over again if given the chance. If given the chance. If given the chance what am I supposed to say, that I would love you less? Why would I. Why should I. I loved the amount I loved. I loved the way I loved. That it is now bricks piled high upon my chest is less regret and more kismet.

Sometimes love breaks.

And sometimes only one of us
gets out before it does.

Sisyphus

When I am feeling noble—and lying to
myself—I declare that we were Sisphyus
and love was our boulder.

When I am feeling vengeful—and still lying
to myself—I contend that I was Sisyphus
and you were the boulder.

When I am feeling introspective—and tired of lying
to myself—I admit that I was both Sisyphus
and the boulder.

When I am feeling tired—and brutally honest
with myself—I acknowledge that I was and ever am
all three of Sisyphus, the boulder, and the mountain.

I am the carrier of my burdens.

I am the burden.

And I am the thing
that I must overcome.

Both You and Peace

I had to draw a line
in the sand.

And I'm sorry
that I could not find a way
to have both you
and peace
on my side of it.

On My Wall

I don't flip houses, but I flip words. You say you miss me, and I rip out the period and replace it with an exclamation point. I slide it back a little bit, though, so I can add a "so much." I change it to all caps. I stretch each letter to ten feet tall. I italicize it, I underline it. I polish it, I frame it.

By the time I ask you about it, you've already forgotten you ever said it.

And I

have hung it

on

my wall.

Reappraised

I sold my love to you so cheaply because
you convinced me that was the most
I would ever get for it.

I got it reappraised.

Turns out
you can't
afford it.

I Wish You Really Had It

I wish you really had it. My heart, I mean, my heart. I wish you had it like a fish in a tank, where you could see what makes it struggle, where you could see what makes it thrive. Where you could see the way it beats harder when you're near. The way it pounds, the way it races. And where you could see the bruises. The cracks, the holes, the blood. The hurt, I wish you could see the hurt, I wish you had to see the hurt.

I wish you really had it.

And I really wish
you didn't.

Over This

I joke that my therapist picks up her pen every time I say your name. That she's keeping a tally of how many times I say it. It might be in the hundreds, is probably in the thousands. If she's tired of it, she doesn't let on, she can't let on, which is why that's the only place I still say it.

Nobody else wants to hear it. Nobody else wants my heart to still be broken. Some of that is kindness I'm sure, but some of it isn't.

Can I blame them? I probably can't blame them.

I want me
to be over this too.

Meant to Be

I know that we
were meant to be,
but it's hard for me to believe
we were meant to be
this.

Memories Included

House for sale, fully furnished, memories included!

Beautiful granite countertops on which I sat and read him crossword clues while he made me pancakes. Dark wood floors—unscratched!—where he spun me 'round and 'round while old Bee Gees records played. (Records also included!) Comfy black sofa where he first told me he loved me, complete with two gorgeous purple pillows I cried into months later when he changed his mind. (Don't worry, no damage!) (No damage to the pillows, I mean, no damage to the pillows.) Working electric fireplace guaranteed to warm your bones, but it might not warm your heart, it shows no sign of warming hearts. The bed, you can have the bed, I have nothing to say about the bed except it has four posts, a mattress, I drown in it, I've drowned in it. Garage fits two cars, but it fits one even better, don't worry, it fits one even better.

I hope it brings you joy, I hope you
burn it to the ground.

(I should have. I should have.)

It Doesn't

Missing you doesn't mean I forgive you
any more than
your silence means you're sorry.

Burn This One

This was sweet once. Me, writing my silly stories. You, fighting your silly wars. Tying our weights to all the wrong things, like words could save us, like bullets could. Like there was something here worth saving. What were we that we are not now. I still clutch my pen, you still clutch your gun. We just fight for things that are not each other.

When I said I loved you, I meant I wanted to. When I say I wanted to, I mean despite it all, I chose to.

Burn this one, go ahead and burn it.

I already did.

Dead Things

I buried our love in the dirt out back.

In the middle of the night, it calls to me.

Maybe dead things
don't know
they're dead.

The Far Away

I was mistaken in thinking
you couldn't hurt me from far away.

It turns out the far away
is what hurts me
most.

A Secret

Love is a secret the stars whispered
in our ears each night.

And I kept it.

I kept it even if
you didn't.

I Think You Know

My wanting you is tired. It curls up
inside of me, and oh, it is small, oh,
it did not used to be this small. I feel
the waning weight of it and think,
*I have wrestled yesterdays bigger
than this.* And I have—I live in
their shadow. (I did not win.)

If words alone could have saved us—

I think you know.

I think you know.

Free Trial

I got a free trial of love, but
I didn't cancel it in time.

And oh, I can't even tell you

how much

it cost me.

In My Dream

In my dream you ask me if I'm
gone and I say *no, I'm right here,
you're the one who's gone.* You
laugh. You laugh and you say,
look at me. You laugh and you
say, *how can I be gone?*

And I echo it back, I echo it back.

I look at you and I say,

how can you be gone?

I Keep Singing

I've watched enough medical shows to know that
sometimes you can't cut out the bad without
risking something good.

Sometimes they keep the patient awake on the table
during brain surgery and tell them to keep talking.

To keep singing.

I keep singing.

Just to make sure
that in losing you
I'm not also losing
me.

I Am Leaving That Piece Here

He asks why I have my shoes on, but I don't know, I don't remember putting them on. Both of us notice the suitcase at the same time, the one my two hands, I suppose, have packed without my knowledge. I am wearing a raincoat and I see now storm clouds gather; the thing in me that wants to go must have checked the forecast. You touch my hand but have already forgotten how to hold it, or I have forgotten how to let you. You kiss me, an ordinary kiss, but I call it a goodbye kiss in my head. Do you know I call it that. Do you know it is that. Do you know I don't want it to be. Do you know it is raining now. Do you know I am breaking now. Do you know when I woke this morning I watched you sleep for twenty minutes and imagined loving you for twenty years.

It isn't enough, though. Twenty minutes, twenty years. It isn't enough and it is raining now.

My hand is on the door. My foot is on the threshold. My eyes are on the sky. I love you. I love you.

I am leaving that piece here.

Island

The summer I loved you, the river couldn't hold all the rain. Do you remember the way the street flooded. Do you remember smiling down at me and saying that the sky had gifted us an island. We made plans, half-joking, to use sticks to spell *don't save us* outside in the backyard. We made plans, half-serious, to toss our phones into the rising water so nothing could make us less of an island. We dragged the comforter downstairs and made a fort beneath the couch cushions, and you loved me, and I loved you.

Do you remember, do you remember.

You loved me, and

I loved you, and

nobody

could save us.

When It Tells Me

If a tree falls in the forest, and
nobody is there to hear it, I will
still always believe it.

When it tells me that it fell,

and when

it tells me that

it hurt.

My Poem

This is *my* poem, and in it, no one dies young. Cars swerve at the last second. Bullets fall to the ground, impotent, the second they leave the barrel. Knives are all rubber. Angry words die in throats, decompose, regrow as sweet ones. There's no such thing as an endangered animal—they all live happy, they all live free, they all live. Everyone has enough. Enough what? Enough. Everyone falls in love, and no one falls back out of it.

Women walk home at night without their keys tucked between their fingers, and we stopped global warming in time—we cared enough.

Maybe that's all this world is, here in my poem—

we care enough.

Goldmine

I put on my helmet, I pick up my pickaxe. (By which I mean I remind myself it's better this way and pick up my pen.) I go into this wound like it's a mine and I'm searching for gold, but I'm just looking for poetry. Chiseling it from the walls of hurt. Collecting it in buckets like it was ever meant to see the light.

My heart is the canary.

It tells me when it's time to go.

It says this place

will kill me.

Over Me

I have not stopped
choosing you,

but I have stopped
choosing you
over me.

You Didn't Mind

When something falls / I try to catch it / I don't want it to break / I don't want to break it / when I fell / you didn't try to catch me / you didn't mind me breaking / you didn't mind breaking me.

I won't chase after
the things / that don't want me
anymore.

Nor will I chase after
the things / that want me but
are cowards.

Shadow Boy

In my memories you are not real. Shadow boy.
Blurred boy. Ghost boy. Sometimes you have eyes,
sometimes you have lips, depending on the memory.
You always have a laugh, somehow you always have
a laugh. In one you have one hand. In one you
have both. In one you have nothing but
a heartbeat. a heartbeat. a heartbeat.

In one you have kindness.

In one you have cruelty.

In one you forget
to ever come back.

To Live One

I have lived whole lives
in your absence,
but I would give them all back
to live one
in your presence.

i do not carry your heart with me
(after e.e. cummings)

i do not carry your heart with me (i thought i carried your heart with me) i am always without it (where did i lose it, how did i lose it) and whatever i do in this life is because you left me (the broken things, the brilliant things)

i do not fear my fate (for i no longer believe in fate) and every world in which i walk is one without you in it (i was wrong to think the world was you and you, the world) and the moon says i was mistaken in thinking it meant you and the sun says i misheard your name within the song it tried to sing

here is the deepest secret everyone knows but me (here is the tangled root of a felled tree in a dying forest beneath a cursed sky in this life we thought we'd build together;which does not grow, will never again grow) and this is the wonder that's keeping the stars from shining

i do not carry your heart with me (i thought i carried your heart with me)

The One That Left

You're not
the one
that got away,
you're just
the one
that left.

Or You Were Too Small for It

You tried on my love for size,
but I see now it
was too big for you.

Acts of God or Foolishness

I am a less fragile thing now than
the one you held. I am neither
unbreakable nor unbroken,
but I have to be dropped
from a higher height these days
for it to make a dent. I need sweeter
words, I need softer warmth, I need
surer arms to hold me. I won't break for
uncertain arms anymore. Insurance doesn't
cover acts of God or foolishness; I had to pay
out of pocket for the ways you wrecked me.

But now I will not hurt for less than love.

And if it's love, I will not

hurt for it.

Not a Single Goddamn Summer

We die young. We get one autumn, one winter, one spring, not a single goddamn summer. I never touch you in July, and you never hold me in August. It's a tragedy but nobody calls it that. They say whirlwind, they say fling. I say things too but you don't hear them. We are past listening, past hearing, past healing.

We die young.

You bury us alive and I
dig us up dead.

You say you miss me and I
stop believing in the universe
when you don't come back.

A Good Thing You Touched

You tried to wash your hands of me, but I hope I
never come off. I hope you mark every good
thing you touch with the memory that I was a
good thing you touched. I want to be the ink
that explodes onto the money you thought
you got away with. Are you proud of what
you got away with?

You may be tangled in my fishing line
memories, but I am a hook in your chest.

On nights heartbreak won't
let me sleep, it brings me solace to think
maybe cowardice won't let you.

Better Safe than Sorry

Is it enough that Hades loved her? Is it? Can it
be? Can I let it be? (I am trying, I am trying.)
Who among us does not want to be loved so
much that someone would split the ground
beneath our feet to keep us? (You.) Who among
us does not want to be kept? (You.) I want badly
to be kept, but you keep me very badly. When
you split the ground beneath my feet, it is only
so that I am on one side and you are on the
other. It is only so that I can't reach you.

You look for exit signs everywhere
we go, saying it's better safe than sorry.

I just look at you because
I have already chosen sorry.

All I Hear

I don't hear your voice
in quiet moments anymore.

All I hear is silence, but—

I still think of it as yours.

All That Matters

Sometimes I wonder
who you've become
in the years since we
last spoke, but I guess
all that matters is that
you didn't become
someone who
came back.

Me? Love?

Me? Love? No I don't do that anymore, no I
don't want that anymore, no I don't let that
rule the heart of me anymore. Me? Love?
No I've tried that, no I've died for that, no
I've bent over backward for lies that taste
like that. Me? Love? No I've lost that, no I've
paid the cost of that, no I've spent too long
trying to foster that and —

me? love?

Only now if you love.

Because I've been alone in that.

I've been waiting by the phone for that.

And still as yet I have not ever come close
to being shown that.

On My Skin

I fell in love with a man
with secrets in his hands,
and now they're on my skin.

I am still no closer
to understanding them
but now I carry them, too.

The Prize

We are not a love story, we are
a war that I've been waging.

I'm winning now.

I just didn't expect the prize
to be peace
instead of
you.

It Isn't the Same

Some days I am still so mad at you I could scream, but instead I just write poetry. It isn't the same, but then again, what is. I imagine a world where you love me without leaving, but in it, I leave instead. Even in make believe, I can't make myself believe in us anymore. We have spent more time looking at each other's backs than we have looking into each other's eyes. We have spent more time keeping each other in the dark than we have holding each other in it.

I pretend that in the silence
you are screaming out my name.

Because in every line of every poem

I am screaming out

yours.

I Hope This Email Finds You
(after Skyler Saunders)

I hope this email finds you on a boat with spotty service. I hope it finds you three months after I sent it and for a second, when you read it, the taste of my name tangles with the whiskey on your tongue. I hope it tastes more sweet than bitter. I hope it tastes like missing.

I hope this email finds you with sunshine on your skin instead of shrapnel. I hope it finds you tanned instead of bruised. I hope it finds you whole. I hope it finds you free. I hope it finds you alive, oh god I hope it finds you alive.

I hope this email finds you in all the ways I couldn't. I hope it fights to reach you, and I hope you know

>   why I couldn't anymore.

All the Good

Maybe he broke my heart open
hoping all the good inside of it
would spill out onto him.

Maybe he wouldn't have bothered
breaking a lesser heart.

Nothing but Ghosts

In a dream I fly out west and knock on your
door and nobody answers. I ask the neighbor
if she's seen you and she says, *honey, that
house has been empty for years*, she says,
*honey, the only ones living there
have been ghosts*.

Ghosts, nothing but ghosts. Ghosts laughing,
ghosts dancing. Ghosts saying it's love, ghosts
saying it's not. Ghosts leaving, ghosts pleading,
ghosts on the floor bleeding.

In a dream you were never real and
neither were we.

Of all the goddamn dreams why
was this the one that had to
come true.

What Love Is

I used to say
if that's not love
then I don't know what
love is.

It turns out
I don't know what
love is.

The Thing We Could Have Been

I mind less that you broke
the thing we were
and more that you broke
the thing we could have been.

This Is How I Keep You

Things don't hurt you the same way they hurt me.

I can count on one hand the number of times I heard you say my name, while yours was and ever has been every word but amen in every one of my prayers.

This is how I keep you —

tucked between my clasped fingers
   beneath my bowed head.

This is how I keep you —

locked inside a forgiveness
   I can't give you if you're not sorry.

If you don't open the box, the cat is both
alive and dead.

If I don't ever talk to you again, you both
still love me and you don't.

This is how I keep you —

like the loudest silence.

Like the quietest
                scream.

The Cracks Inside of It

Sometimes I'm a body and sometimes I'm the girl inside of it. Sometimes I'm the heart inside of her. Sometimes I'm the cracks inside of it.

Einstein said either everything's a miracle or nothing is but that means if you and me were a miracle then somehow you leaving has to be too.

My neighbor sits in his parked car in his driveway every day and listens to old love songs, and I wonder if he can't bring himself to go inside because it's empty or because it isn't.

Is he the one with cracks inside his heart or is he the one making them.

I love you. I still say your name sometimes. I finally believe you're never coming back. I finally believe

    I don't want you to.

It's a Long Story

When people ask about us I say it's a long story like I don't want to tell it but I do. I want to tell them how we met and I want to tell them how you left.

I want to tell them every time our paths cross I love you a little harder and you hurt me a little deeper.

I want to tell them I almost called you last night but didn't because if it's hell not hearing your voice it's a different kind of hell hearing it tell me goodbye.

I want to tell them I think I'll spend my whole life wondering if you meant anything you said to me and if you ever wish you hadn't said it or if you ever wish you could've kept it.

I want to tell them about the first night, and I want to tell them about the last night, and I want to tell them I loved you. I want to tell them you loved me.

It's what I want to tell them.

Not what I can.

Braver

I can't say for sure that
anything you might have said
would have been better than
this silence, but

I can say for sure that
it would have
been braver.

You Leaving In My Eye

I'm not crying, that's just dust, that's just the
sun, that's just you leaving in my eye. Tell me
how we survive this. Not you and me but you.
and me.

My heart keeps insisting we ran out of pages
before we ran out of story so I give us endings
we didn't have, which is to say, I give us one.

No one tells you that sometimes heaven
comes at a price and that price
                          is
                                    hell.

Hey Taylor

Hey Taylor,

I think he knows. That this is the last time, that we can't begin again, that everything has changed. I tell him, *you can call it what you want but that won't change what it is.* (Treacherous.) (Haunted.) He tells me, *you need to calm down.* He tells me, *you belong with me.*

Hey Taylor,

I wish you would tell me why I can't shake it off. Why the very first night I had to fight the urge to run. Why he's just on the other side of the door but I can't bring myself to breathe, let alone speak now.

Hey Taylor,

You said 'tis the damn season but I guess you didn't mean for a love story. I know all too well it's time to go so don't blame me if I almost do.

This is me trying not to.

Honey

Honey I fought for this, got lost
for this, saw most of my heart
broken off for this, honey I tried
for this, truth be told lied for this,
late at night quietly cried for this,
honey I believed in this, begged
on my knees for this, hugged my
own waist as I grieved for this,
honey, honey, honey, I can't

do this anymore. Can't wait by
the phone anymore. Can't wish
you'd be someone you're not
anymore. Can't wish you'd be
someone

you never were

anymore.

The Lions of Tsavo

I stuff my heart like the man-eating lions in the
Field Museum — jaw open, mid-roar. (Did they
really do all the things they said they did; did they
mean to?) Stick it in a glass case rigged with
alarms and a superfluous sign that says *Don't
Touch*. Look closely you can see that it is held
together by pins. Look closely you can see
all the places where it broke.

Men with nice smiles buy replicas from the
souvenir shop and can't even tell
the difference.

Can't even tell
they don't beat.

Can't even tell
you're not in there.

Can't even tell
I'm not either.

You Coward

I've been checking obituaries
again. Reading off names,
thinking about how every loss
is someone's. Wondering if
your loss will still be mine, all
these years later. Wondering if
anything short of seeing
your name on these pages
would make this feel
done, would let me move on.

I still loved you on the nights
you wouldn't let me call it that.

Call me, you
               coward.

Closer

We looked at the same love but it
was like an embroidery hoop where
I only saw the beauty of us and you
only saw the tangled mess.

Neither of us can say we
truly saw it for what it was, but
I still think I
came closer.

Unheard

California breaks my heart. I step off the plane and the earth quakes but nobody else seems to feel it. No I'm sorry that's just the tired talking, that's just the retrograde talking, that's just the holes inside of me I keep falling in talking. I don't miss you if I don't think of you but California makes me think of you, just like ferries do, just like starry skies do, just like most days and most nights do. That doesn't mean it's still love, just that I'm still littered with what ifs.

I take solace in the fact
that I left nothing unsaid
regardless that you left it all

unheard.

What Comes After

I am not afraid
of love, I am
afraid of what
comes after.

By My Fingertips

Still now years later when I draw love
I draw myself dangling by my fingertips
from the edge of a cliff.

I never know where to draw you, though.

Were you standing at the top,
could you have pulled me up?

Or were you standing at the bottom,
could you have caught me?

I guess it doesn't matter
what you *could* have done.

For Anything

I won't ask you for anything
you can't give anymore.

An explanation, an apology.

Kindness, your heart.

I won't ask you for anything
you don't have anymore.

Five Years Ago Today

Snapchat asks me if I remember what I was doing five years ago today and goddammit I was trying not to, all I'm ever doing is trying not to. I know I was sitting on the floor of a house I don't go to anymore, calling a dog who isn't alive anymore, in love with a man I don't know anymore. I look at the photos anyway. I watch the video. I watch that dog run toward me, tripping over her feet, all joy. All glee. She puts my whole hand in her mouth and I say, *gentle. Gentle.*

Five years from now if Snapchat asks me
if I remember what I was doing five years
ago — today — I'll know

my whole heart was in my mouth
and blood was dripping down my throat
and god none of this
was gentle.

Things We Didn't Mean

In the end,
we both said things
we didn't mean.

I said
I never wanted to see you again.

You said
you'd always love me.

The Place I Live

Nowadays I paint myself in
my favorite colors instead
of yours.

When I finally come home
to myself, I want to like
the place
I live.

Why Aren't You

I have reached for stars in the sky
less out of reach than you.

I tell myself it is better to be
the aftermath than the war but it is
too quiet here; not enough hearts
are beating here; everyone can hear me
screaming here.

The calendar said last week was spring
but now the flowers say it too.

The geese are flying home
so why aren't you.

No Rhyme or Reason

I have not touched you in years so I wrote you
into this poem; it's the only way I still know how
to feel you. Honey you feel like everything I
never got the chance to say. Honey you feel like
the space between the last time I heard your
voice and forever. The haunting of unrequited
wanting. A rending of an ending.

Someone told me it's not poetry unless
it rhymes or unless
there's a reason for it.

But I loved you without rhyme.

I loved you without
                        reason.

Unburdened

Unburdened of my love and trust,

tell me —

    do you feel

        free

            enough.

Come to Your Senses

I won't lie to you, I don't wish you well. I
wish the taste of me on your tongue. I wish
the sound of my laugh in your ears. I wish
the scent of my skin in your nose. I wish
the sight of my wanting you in your eyes
every time you close them.

I wish the feel of me in your arms. On
your fingertips. Across your body.

I don't wish you well, I wish you
would come to my senses.

If you did, you'd find me
in all of them.

Wasted

As for us, we were
drunk on love, wasted
on love, no —

love
was wasted
on us.

Some of It

I have never loved
myself less than when
I loved you.

And while most of
that's on me—

some of it's on
you, too.

Too Clean

Bones break, hearts don't.

Hearts give out (they can't keep doing this.) Hearts murmur (and we don't listen.) Hearts skip beats (and we'll never get those back.)

Hearts are a muscle and muscles don't break.

Muscles tear.

Muscles rip.

Muscles rupture.

I just want to be clear because a break sounds too clean

for what this was.

A Name

I gave love
a name it doesn't answer to,
and now it won't come back.

(I gave it yours.)

Takeout

I put love in a paper bag with a fork,
a knife, two napkins. (I know love can
get messy.)

I leave it on the takeout shelf but
the person who said they wanted it
never comes to get it.

It is still on that shelf, if anyone
else wants it. It is paid in full.

(I paid the price.) (*I
paid the price.*)

Small Yellow Bird

I hit
a small yellow bird
with my car yesterday
because neither of us
saw the other
until it was too late.

He could have
survived it.

I tell myself
he could have
survived it.

And I do not go back
to check because
if I do, I will no longer
be able
to lie to myself.

No Reckoning

Maybe there will be no reckoning. Maybe the
seas won't boil, maybe they'll all be acquitted
of their crimes, they who know what they did,
they who we all saw what they did. Maybe the
next ark will have room for all of us, and instead
of two by two we will march up that plank as we
came into this world — alone. As we will leave
this world — alone. As we have been but for
fleeting moments here and there as we existed
in this world — alone.

Maybe the someday
I imagine you'll regret this
won't come.

Maybe that really was our goodbye.

(That absence of one.)

Band-Aid on a Corpse

You saying you're
sorry now would be like
putting a Band-Aid on a corpse.

Do not dig up
what I've already
mourned.

3 AM

It's 3 AM and I'm alone but I'm not lonely. I'm awake. I'm awake. I'm so awake I'm not sure I was ever asleep. I will still want more than this sometimes, but never less. Never less. Tell me how hands that have held the world can ever hold anything less.

There is a piece of me not here and there is a piece of you not there but sweetheart most of me is here and most of you is there.

I have nowhere to lay flowers.

So I water them instead.

Night & Day

As the sun sets with you
beside me, more than night
falls;

as the sun rises with you
gone, more than day
breaks.

The Question

The question is not
who am I
if you don't love me,
it's who am I
if I let
you not loving me
change
who I am.

Just One

You think you can't be found guilty if
you're not here to stand trial? You think
because there's no extradition from your
hidey-hole you get to pretend this didn't
happen, you didn't love me, you didn't
hurt me and then hurt me and then hurt
me again? (You hurt me more times
than you ever loved me.)

When I started to love you I thought to
myself, *what's the worst that could happen*,
and I thought heartbreak but I didn't think this.

I didn't think the absence of answers could
hurt more than one I didn't want to hear.

I want to hear one, just one.

I want you to believe
I deserve one.

I Know

If love is patient

& love is kind,

I know

this was

not love.

Ten Years

I wanted to call you up and tell you
today is ten years since the night we
met, but then I remembered that
just because we have some kind of past
doesn't mean we have any kind of future.

(You made sure of that.)

I wanted to call you up and tell you
I had the stupidest goddamn epiphany
last night that shattered rhymes with
mattered and how that felt like halfway
to an answer I've been trying to find
for over half these ten years.

Mostly I wanted to call you up and ask you
if my heart's still beating beneath your
floorboards, telltale —

keeping a rhythm some part of me hopes
some part of you still dances to.

Interrogation

Heartbreak is
an interrogation where
the only answer
my heart knows to give
is love,
but I keep hurting it
and demanding
it give
a different
one.

How Much Else

I still run my fingertips down
the spine of us, but I don't open
us anymore.

My scabs have all graduated
to scars; I finally stopped
picking at them.

I don't say your name these days, but
other people have it, and now I can say
theirs without it coming out in pieces.

When I see the moon my
first thought is that it's beautiful
instead of wondering where you are.

They said it would take time, and
they're right, it did.

I do not think
I need to tell you
how much else
it took.

Winter Soldier

Mercury's in retrograde so I dreamt you again.

Every time I think missing you is gone, it's just
lurking around the corner or hiding under a
blanket or waiting for some song to play like
it's got a list of trigger words and I'm Bucky
Barnes with a Winter Soldier in me that
does nothing but still love you.

I'm not making you the bad guy in this,
but I am making you

the coward.

A Wonder

You broke my whole heart.

I've spent years repainting walls and
replacing frames when really I've got
structural damage. I've got chasms, I've
got cracks, it's a wonder I'm still standing.

I chose a light grey for the walls.

I chose not to hang our pictures.

It's a wonder I'm
still standing.

The Only Reason

When I'm scared my instinct
is still to reach for your hand, but
these days I'd rather
cut off my own
than reach for yours.

(It may yet come to that.)

Missing is a hole I didn't think I was
still fool enough to fall into but
I am writing this from
the bottom of it.

I am the only reason
this was ever a love story.

You are the only reason
it's a tragedy now.

Dirty Breaks

I don't do clean breaks, I
do them dirty.

I leave my sweatshirt in
your car, I text you
every time I drink.

If it's between a scalpel and
a sledgehammer, I always choose
the sledgehammer.

Some days hurting
hurts less than
healing.

Some days hurting you
heals me more than
forgiveness.

This Message

I scream heartbreak into a bottle and
throw it out to sea because
no one else wants to hear it.

I'm sorry to
whoever gets this message.

I'm sorry to
whoever truly gets it.

This week would be six years, but instead,
it's three years of something else.

You said all the things
you knew I needed to hear;

if only you had meant the things
I needed you to mean.

A Warmth You Never Had

I have kept you alive
in these poems long past
the point you should have
been dead to me.

I have put beats into
your silent heart; steady
breath into your lungs.

I have given you a warmth
you never had, in
here, in the words
that have held me

all the nights that you
have not.

CONTENTS

2016	128
2023	288
(I Needed You.)	49
(Say It.)	101
3 AM	427
A Broken Thing	224
A Cure	158
A Good Thing You Touched	385
A Handful of Roses	108
A Hell of a Thing	79
A Hollow Victory	240
A Home	220
A Mess	338
A Moat	226
A Name	422
A Problem	327
A Reminder	202
A Secret	366
A Sign	229
A Someday	201
A Thing That Goes	135
A Thing That Happened	324
A Thousand Love Poems in a Trench Coat	282
A Warmth You Never Had	440
A Weakness	59
A Wonder	436
A World	88
About You	316
Acts of God or Foolishness	383
All for Me	274
All I Ever Seem to Do	48
All I Have Left	198
All I Hear	387
All I Take Back	19
All or None	336

All or Nothing	159
All That Matters	388
All the Brighter	291
All the Good	394
All the Same	170
All You Did	83
Already Broken	173
Already Gone	18
An Ocean	262
And the Phoenix Said	308
And to Think	342
And Yet, and Still	65
Anything But	205
Anyway	150
Anyway, I Reach	152
Apart	269
As Though	10
At the Bottom of the Sea	330
Backpack	81
Band-Aid on a Corpse	426
Be Brave	244
Believe	134
Bent	21
Better	118
Better Now	297
Better Safe than Sorry	386
Between the Lines	191
Binary Stars	225
Bittersweet	17
Blame	100
Bloom	292
Both You and Peace	355
Boy of a Man	13
Bravely	163
Braver	401
Break Down	3
Broken Glass	156

Broken In	190
Bulldozer	93
Burn This One	363
Burning Bridges	214
But It Was	46
But Mostly	119
By My Fingertips	410
California	96
Can't	112
Can't Be Sure	328
Catch Me	261
Closer	407
Come and Get It	310
Come to Your Senses	418
Coming to Terms	62
Cracks	289
Darker	246
Dead End	115
Dead Things	364
Demons	9
Detonated	130
Devastation	217
Dirty Breaks	438
Do You	86
Doomed	54
Drain	85
Eighth Wonder	264
Ending	122
Endlessly Endlessly	178
Enough Things	162
Eulogy	172
Every Letter	192
Every Night	20
Every Poem	106
Everything	45
Except, Perhaps	76
Eyes Wide Open	294

Ferry	8
Fiction	257
Firsts	215
Five Years Ago Today	412
Fix It	153
Flags	174
Flattened	36
For a Long Time	303
For Anything	411
For Me	4
For You	75
For You	227
Forever	107
Forgive Me	349
Free Trial	368
From Afar	312
From the Beginning	142
From the Sparrows	140
Frozen	211
Ghosts	57
Goldmine	375
Good to You	64
Grasping	271
Grenade	315
Happier	109
Hard to Love	254
He Doesn't Realize	137
Heartbreak	58
Heavy	187
Hell If I Know	110
Hello, Love	104
Hello, World	82
Here's to the Nights	305
Hey Taylor	403
High School Math	212
Honey	404
Hope	38

Hourglass	34
House on Fire	286
How	24
How Long	339
How Much	223
How Much Else	434
How Much More	309
How Not To	133
Howl	255
I Am Leaving That Piece Here	371
I Can't Hear You	195
I Cannot	37
I Could Have	105
I Didn't Mean To	50
i do not carry your heart with me	380
I Exist	35
I Go, Too	60
I Hope This Email Finds You	393
I Hope, I Hope, I Hope	252
I Keep Singing	370
I Know	431
I Live Around It	268
I Pretend	1
I Smile Like This	67
I Still Believe	334
I Still Look at You	200
I Thank You	16
I Think I Used To	11
I Think You Know	367
I Wish You Really Had It	358
I'm Convinced	131
I'm Sorry	138
If Given the Chance	353
If It Could	91
Imagine	283
In Here	182
In My Dream	369

In This House	311
In This One	250
Instead of Peace	346
Interrogation	433
Island	372
Isn't It Cruel	98
It Doesn't	362
It Doesn't Have to Be	279
It Has Taken Some Time	120
It Isn't the Same	392
It Knew	56
It Thinks It	251
It's a Long Story	400
It's Complicated	238
It's Like This	71
Jeopardy	188
Just a Little Bit	14
Just One	430
Kamikaze Love	304
Kept	111
Kites	43
Later	5
Less	235
Less Joy	40
Let Me Show You	23
Liars	272
Life Lessons	237
Lightning in a Bottle	293
Looking	228
Looking for You	166
Lost is Lost	306
Love and Hurt	321
Magic Trick	275
Make a Liar of Me	280
Make Do	165
March and You	149
Maybe I Was Right	350

Maybe I Was Wrong	197
Maybe I'm Wrong	260
Maybe Mars	233
Maybe Someday	245
Me? Love?	389
Meany to Be	360
Memories	216
Memories Included	361
Memorized	313
Mercy	267
Metaphors	213
Michelangelo	196
Miracles	161
Mistaken	230
My Happy Place	26
My Heart Breaks Here	145
My Poem	374
My Some	298
Never Let It Be Said	181
Never Nobody	179
Night & Day	428
No	123
No Easier	325
No Hitch, No Falter	265
No Promises	47
No Reckoning	425
No Rhyme or Reason	416
Nobody	204
Nobody's Better	44
Not a Single Goddamn Summer	384
Not Enough	239
Not Sorry	121
Not That Far	299
Not Yet	97
Nothing	146
Nothing but Ghosts	395
Nothing Here	33

Nothing to Be Proud Of	281
Now I Am	302
Now I See	177
Now I Wonder	132
On a Beach	78
On Both of Us	248
On My Skin	390
On My Wall	356
One of Them	247
One Small Word	193
Only One	51
Only the Beginning	184
Or You Were Too Small for It	382
Origin Story	176
Otherwise	169
Our Blue Moon	95
Ours	164
Over Me	376
Over This	359
Over You	87
Phoenix	94
Pieces	259
Pretenders	278
Prey	124
Proud	175
Pulse	143
Quiet	125
Razed	77
Reappraised	357
Reclaim It	28
Regrets	168
Remember	52
Remember Me	92
Ruins	222
Sad Little Poems	273
Sadness	333
Safe Mode	53

Save Me	42
Say It's the Sea	243
Seashells	32
Shadow	287
Shadow Boy	378
Ships in the Night	25
Shouting Us	203
Sieve	68
Silent	73
Silent Film	207
~~Simply Impossible~~ Impossibly Simple	167
Sisyphus	354
Small Yellow Bird	424
Smaller	154
So I Walk	347
So Long	351
So Much Space	348
Solar Flare	343
Some of It	420
Someone Else	74
Something Lasting	27
Something That Can Leave You	344
Sometimes I Think	126
Stay	160
Still	89
Still Always	319
Still On It	322
Still There	332
Still You	114
Stolen	147
Takeout	423
Tell Me	72
Tell Me	277
Ten Years	432
That Scene	7
That Was Me	263
That's All There Is	63

That's It	155
That's What I Wanted to Tell You	55
The Audacity of Heartbreak	352
The Beginning	194
The Better Question	29
The Cracks Inside of It	399
The Dark	295
The Elephant in the Room	157
The Far Away	365
The Fool	180
The Foundation	113
The Hard Way	329
The Hardest Part	331
The Hardest Truths	148
The Kind I Cannot Win	12
The Kindest Thing	270
The Last Thing	290
The Least	266
The Lions of Tsavo	405
The Nerve	210
The Ocean's Memory	241
The One That Left	381
The Ones That Stay	300
The Only One, the Lonely One	31
The Only Reason	437
The Only Story	70
The Place I Live	414
The Prize	391
The Question	429
The Rest of Me	284
The Sky	256
The Thing We Could Have Been	397
The Things Worth Keeping	61
The Way That I Hold On	144
The Why	335
These Scars	84
These Words	30

They Were Bright	206
Things We Didn't Mean	413
This	136
This and Not That	285
This Heart of Mine	127
This Heartbreak	186
This Is How I Keep You	398
This Is Not Benevolence	253
This Is What I Remember	15
This Message	439
This Poem	209
To Feel Alive	231
To Life	139
To Live One	379
To the Light	236
Too Clean	421
Too Much	242
Too Soon	183
Tsunami	276
Tumbleweed	219
Tunnel	189
Two Months	232
Two Settings	208
Two Years Ago	103
Unburdened	417
Unfinished Business	340
Unforgivable	69
Unheard	408
Unless	314
Unsure	141
Waiting	117
Waiting	185
Waiting	337
Wasted	419
Waves	90
What a Waste	307
What Comes After	409

What Do You Give Up	171
What Has Changed	102
What I Deserve	6
What I Wanted	22
What If	39
What If You Came Back	41
What It Doesn't Say	2
What It Was	320
What Love Is	396
What We Are Now	326
What Would You Do	345
What's Best for Me	129
Whatever It Takes	296
When It Tells Me	373
When They Ask Me	341
Where You Are	218
Whether or Not	323
Which One of Us	151
Whiskey Drunk	199
Why Aren't You	415
Wide as the World	234
Winter Soldier	435
Winter Solstice	116
With Patience	249
Wreckage	221
Wrecking Ball	66
Wrong	317
You Could	301
You Coward	406
You Didn't Mind	377
You Leaving In My Eye	402
You Won't Know This	318
Your Ghost	99
Your Heart	80
Yours	258

ABOUT THE AUTHOR

Kristina Mahr is an author and poet who lives in the suburbs of Chicago with her family, friends, and small herd of rescue animals. In her spare time she enjoys drinking tall glasses of iced tea, reading, and waking up at the crack of dawn every weekend to watch the Premier League.

You can find more information about her other poetry collections, as well as her fiction novels, on her website at:

www.kristinamahr.com

Made in United States
Orlando, FL
07 September 2023